LOOK FOR YOURSELF

THE SCIENCE AND
ART OF SELF-REALIZATION

LOOK FOR YOURSELF

THE SCIENCE AND
ART OF SELF-REALIZATION

Douglas E. Harding

InnerDirections
PUBLISHING
Encinitas, California

InnerDirections Publishing

THE INNER DIRECTIONS FOUNDATION
P.O. Box 231486
Encinitas, California 92023
Phone: 800 545-9118

Printed in Canada on acid-free recycled paper

ISBN 1-878019-01-5

Cover illustration by Michael Green
Book & cover design by Joan Greenblatt

FIRST AMERICAN EDITION
Originally published by The Shollond Trust (1996)
London, England.

Library of Congress Catalog Card Number: 98-60142

It might be good to open our eyes and see.
—THOMAS MERTON

The whole of life lies in the verb to see.
—TEILHARD DE CHARDIN

The word is none other than SEE.
—JAN VAN RUYSBROECK

I see no more than you, but I have trained myself to notice what I see.
—SHERLOCK HOLMES

I see just what all see, nothing more. I see what needs to be seen.
All are seeing God always, but they don't know it.
—RAMANA MAHARSHI

CONTENTS

FOREWORD

This beautifully written spiritual autobiography by a British philosopher and architect is based on a unique insight experienced
early in his life. He has described this experience in a previous book
"On Having No Head," and over the years has elaborated on it. Essentially it is a totally original approach to the eternal question posed by
seers and mystics of all backgrounds: "Who or What Am I?"

Conventional wisdom in this respect is totally misleading and the
cause of all the trouble in the world. In Harding's own words, it is
based on one universal but well-hidden assumption:

> *I am what I look like.* These six little words are big
> enough to cover the whole reason for our plight. They
> say it all. Or, to elaborate somewhat: *I am here, for myself,*
> *what I look like over there, to you* — as if our distance
> made no difference! On this morass you and I try to
> build our lives. No wonder they are cracking up. To
> render them safe and sound we must rebuild them on
> the bedrock of *I am what I see I am here; what you see is*
> *just one of my regional appearances.* I alone, at center, am
> in a position to say what those myriad appearances
> are appearances of, and how different they *all* are from
> the one Reality that's giving rise to them, from what
> I'm looking out of. On this I'm the sole and final
> authority.

Harding's entire work consists of manifold variations on this very theme, which are worthy of careful study and contemplation by lovers of Self-knowledge. Writing and speaking about this for over forty years, Hardings' experiments have found a wide audience. It seems that in the last decade more and more people have sought to understand the absolute necessity to experience for themselves, the "headlessness" which Harding has so eloquently explored all these years.

Though the essays in this book are quite diverse, they all touch the core issue of self-discovery and are bound together by the simple and obvious rediscovery of "oneself," by oneself. And all this is recorded by a true master of English prose, which makes it a double pleasure to peruse.

Robert Powell

PREFACE

This book consists of a selection of the articles I have written over the past forty years. Most of them are revised versions of contributions to *The Middle Way*, *The Mountain Path*, the *Saturday Evening Post*, and a number of other magazines, mostly French. A few, however, have been written in the last year or two, specially for this collection.

On glancing down the Table of Contents, you could well get the impression that here is a miscellany so miscellaneous, a patchwork so patchy, that only the bookbinding holds it together. What on earth could the connection be between Architecture, a Walk in the Forest, Tenderness, and Transubstantiation? Well, you will see. In fact, all the chapters are variations on the theme clearly rung out by the title of the book — LOOK FOR YOURSELF. My hope is that the variety of these variations will help to show how it is that the Ultimate Simplicity of our True Nature is the answer to the infinite complexities of our life and the problem of coping with them.

Read the chapters in any order you fancy. Each, though supported by the others, is self-contained.

Douglas E. Harding
Nacton, Ipswich
ENGLAND

THE
SHORTEST
PATH

The field of religion is huge and in places very wild, but it certainly isn't trackless. It contains all too many paths or ways, some
more like trunk roads and others barely discernible tracks. Every sect,
and indeed every spiritual innovator, hacks a new route through the
jungle and sets up signposts and makes some attempt to draw a map of
the route's twists and turns, its staging posts and rest houses, and to
give some idea of its destination. So many paths there are, criss-cross-
ing or running parallel, converging here and diverging there, and leading — where? That's the question.

A few centuries ago the religious scene was, for the great majority
of people, far less complicated. Comparative religion, and the explosion of literature about the world's faiths — first scholarly and then
popular — more or less covering the whole field, had yet to come. For
nearly everyone nearly everywhere, one's religion was simply that of
one's family and social group from time immemorial. In effect, there
existed only this one true and sacred path. Other religions and sects,
insofar as one heard of them at all, were believed to lead nowhere, or
more likely to some very unholy and unhealthy regions right off the
map.

But nowadays, for increasing numbers of us, the situation is nothing like so clear-cut and simple. We are presented with a fast-growing
and bewildering choice of paths, many if not most of which run through
country in which psychology and psychotherapy and spirituality are
inextricably entangled. Visit a store selling books on religion and al-

lied subjects, and you will see what I mean. There the books are stacked floor to ceiling, thousands and thousands of them. The trouble is that, until you have actually traveled one of the many highways and byways that compete for your patronage, you cannot know where it leads; and when at last you do get to the end of it (after who knows how many years and decades or even lifetimes, if ever you do) you have left it rather late to try any of the others. In that case, how are you to discover which of them all is *your* path, the right one for you and leading to your heart's desire and the ultimate truth, the end of all your troubles?

I'm afraid that what actually happens has nothing to do with deliberate choosing, but is chancy to a degree. One just happens to pick up this wonderful book in a friend's house, or casually meets someone who adores that marvelous teacher, or gets through the post a leaflet about a meeting one really must attend. And so one starts off on a path by a kind of accident, you could say irresponsibly. One is more careful, more wary and exploring, before investing in some kitchen utensil, let alone a suit of clothes or a house.

What can be done about this absurd state of affairs? Is it avoidable? Yes it is, and in this chapter I want to show precisely how.

First we must take a much closer look at the religious map. So far, I have implied that there's no regular pattern to these many paths, that they have little in common and no general direction. In practice, that's not at all true. They all serve one overriding purpose, which is to enable one to get away. The whole reason for a path is to make it easier to go somewhere else, to leave the place one's now at and turn up in another place that's distant in space and time. This blazingly obvious fact isn't revealed to the "objective" student of comparative religion, surveying the whole field from a great height: to him the tangle of paths is all of it given at a safe distance, and accordingly shows no simple pattern common to all paths. But for the serious traveler on the ground, for the committed spiritual seeker — no matter how little or great his "spiritual progress" — the map is always wheel-shaped. He finds himself always HERE at the wheel's hub, and all paths, and in particular the path he's taking, radiate like spokes leading to a rim that's labeled ELSEWHERE [See drawing on next page].

And the questions he asks are: am I traveling in exactly the right direction, and how far off is the goal, and how long will it take to get there?

Questions to which, alas, clear answers are in short supply. How is

the poor traveler to judge? The reputation and popularity of a way are no sure guide to its practicality. In fact, the wider and better paved and well-traveled the beginning of a way or path, the longer and more difficult it is apt to become later on. The going may prove so hard and the hazards so daunting that very few travelers arrive, or claim to have arrived at the goal, whose unimaginable delights are conceived to be proportionate to the rigors of the journey. Indeed one gets the impression that no short, smooth, straight path can lead to any place worth getting to.

We shall presently see that this impression is entirely false, and that such a path does indeed exist, and moreover couldn't be easier to find and to travel. It's our built-in resistance to the obvious that persuades us otherwise.

But before examining — and taking — this shortest of paths, let us look at what amounts to its opposite and reverse, the path which you and I traveled so long ago that we have forgotten it. I think it would be better to speak for myself here and not for you. As we proceed please check how far my story resembles yours.

Let me reconstruct that original journey of mine, as far as I'm able. My story starts at birth. Actually, for myself at no distance from myself, I wasn't born at all, though my parents, distant from me by some inches and feet, naturally had a quite different story to tell. In my own firsthand experience I certainly didn't begin as a baby, or as a human being, or as anything at all. On the contrary, I was this beginningless No-thing or Room or Capacity for those ever-changing things. At first, of course, the things that occupied me were comparatively unorganized, but quite soon they began sorting themselves out into that nourishing breast, those fondling hands, those fascinating little arms and legs and fingers and toes, that gorgeous ball and noisy rattle, those smiling or frowning faces, and so on. And all those impressions — that rich world of tastes and feels and smells and sounds and colors and movements — was all of it presented to me right here, unseparate from me, all coming and going in *my* Space. It's true that more and more things, in ever-increasing variety and degree of organization, kept appearing in this Spaciousness. But I was not one of those things. How could I be — I who was Accommodation for them all? In short, I was still myself, still at home, still with myself and not yet beside myself. Which means I was still sane.

But humankind had designs on my native sanity. As time went by my parents persuaded me to stand aside from myself and take up their viewpoint, to leave home and make the momentous journey from Here where I'm perceived to be No-thing to There where I appear to be a very substantial Some-thing. They taught me that the character staring at me out of my mirror was not who I took him to be — namely, "that baby over there", or "my little friend who lives in the other bathroom behind the glass" — but was someone called Douglas, and indeed was me. With the help of friends and relations they taught me — and the lesson took many years and many tears to learn thoroughly — to "see" myself no longer from where I am but from where they are, as if through their eyes and from their viewpoint.

I was a slow learner. For years I traveled back and forth along that original road of one meter plus, undecided about where finally to take up residence. At times, particularly when playing happily on my own, I was content to stay here at home. At other times, particularly when in company and subject to criticism and therefore much less at ease, I took up my position over there, looking back at myself and "seeing" what I reckoned others were seeing — a complete human being like the rest of the folk around. In fact, of course, this wasn't seeing at all but imagination. Or rather hallucination, inasmuch as I superimposed upon myself at center what belonged at a distance. As the years went by I spent longer and longer out there looking back anxiously at Douglas Harding, and less and less here being Accommodation for others, till in the end I came to live a truly eccentric life as an exile, held as if in a trap or prison so near yet so far from home. A miss was as good as a mile, of course, and in effect I was infinitely estranged from myself. It was as if I had never been at home, had never visited my native land.

If ever a soul was lost in hell, I was that soul. Meister Eckhart tells my story: "No man was ever lost except for the reason that, having once left his Home Ground, he has let himself become too permanently settled abroad. There are many who have sought Light and Truth, but only abroad where they are not. They finally go so far out that they never get back to find their way in again. Nor have they found the Truth, for the Truth is in their Ground, not outside."

Correction: Grace, taking the form of extreme agony and desperation, drove me to breach the walls of my prison and open out the way home. But of course the return journey isn't made once and for all. It takes just about as much practicing as the outward journey did. The seasoned traveler comes to know that road — its length and direction and the means of transport available — very well indeed. Unlike those jailbirds who have settled down to prison life, he's anything but vague about the escape route. His description of the road home runs like this:

It doesn't lead from Here to There, but from There to Here; in other words, it's centripetal and not centrifugal. It's very short, its length being the distance between that face I see in my mirror and the absence-of-face I see here. Or, again, the distance between you over there who are taking in one of my many regional appearances and myself here who is the central Reality which is giving rise to them all. It is very straight, as we shall presently see, and upon it only a very determined untruth seeker could lose his way. Finally, it's easy going, and any number of vehicles and modes of transport stand ready to take the traveler home.

Here is one of them. I look at that face in my hand mirror, noting where it's given, how small it is and how complicated, how old it is, and which way round
it is. And then I let my attention
travel along my outstretched arm
to what lies here at the near end of
it, and I observe that in all respects
it's the opposite of that. Right here I find
the One who is wide awake to himself
as boundless, absolutely clear, and
ageless, and who never, never turns
his back upon anyone or anything.
Here I find — I am — the Hospitality

that finds room for that arm and hand and mirror and face, the face that I keep out there, the face that can never get much nearer to me than that.

"Can I find my Self in a mirror?" asks Ramana Maharshi, and continues: "Because you look outwards you have lost sight of the Self and your vision is external ... Turn your gaze within." Nor is this difficult, he assures us: "It's absurd — the idea that to see other things is easy but to look within is hard. It must be the other way round."

And here's a second method of turning round, a second vehicle for making that one-meter journey.

I hold out my hands about 12 inches apart. Then slowly, slowly I bring them forward *while attending to the interval between them,* till they vanish on either side of me. And I take on; actually become that space, the gap which is visibly no longer a few inches across but infinitely wide and deep.

Those are just two of the countless vehicles that are lined up to take you safely and comfortably across that no-man's-land — around one-meter wide, which separates your appearance over there from your Reality right here. Please try the two vehicles I've described, or find your own. But for God's sake, which is your own sake, don't fail to make that journey. It's the only one that matters. It takes you all the way from what you look like to what you are, namely Capacity aware of itself, and beyond even Awareness to the unknowable Abyss from which Awareness timelessly and effortlessly springs. In short, it sees you Home.

In the end, of course, this most direct and shortest of paths is even shorter and more direct than I have said. It has no length at all. As Maharshi points out, "There is no reaching the Self ... You are already that." After all, it was only a pretence that I could leave myself behind and venture out there to find out what others were making of me. There's no way of escaping from here, because I take Here with me wherever I go. Which is to say that I take No-thing with me, nothing but this Awareness which I am.

And so, in conclusion, the path or way we travel is as long or as short as we care to make it. And all paths, including our meter-long one, finally reduce to no distance at all, seeing that it's impossible to leave or approach Oneself. So it is that, at the end of every genuine spiritual path there lies the realization that the weary traveler never left Home for an instant, and that the way itself, however short or long and arduous, was quite fictional.

THE TRUE SEEING, THE ETERNAL SEEING

Seeing into nothingness is the true seeing, the eternal seeing — SHEN-HUI

This seeing is, quite simply, a matter of turning round the arrow of one's attention. The *Katha Upanishad* puts it this way: "God made the senses turn outwards. Man therefore looks outwards, not into himself. But occasionally a daring soul, desiring immortality, has looked back and found himself."

Contrary, no doubt, to one's first impression, there's no seeing, no experience remotely like this seeing into the nothingness right where one is. Here are five of its unique and immeasurably precious characteristics.

First, though down the centuries this in-seeing has been made out to be the most difficult thing in the world, it's really the easiest. This most cruel of practical jokes, this most impious of pious confidence tricks, has taken in countless earnest seekers. The treasure of treasures they wore themselves out searching for is in fact the most accessible, the most exposed and blatantly obvious of discoveries, brilliantly lit up and on show all the time. The Buddha's description of Nirvana in the Pali Canon, as "visible in this very life, inviting, attractive, accessible," makes perfect sense. So does Zen Master Huang-po's caustic comment that one must be blind drunk not to see this. So does Zen Master Ummon's statement that the *first* step along the path of Zen is to see into our void nature: getting rid of our bad *karma* comes afterwards.

Then there's Ramana's insistence that it's easier to see What and Who we really are than to see a gooseberry in the palm of our hand. All of which means that there are no preconditions for this essential in-seeing. To oneself one's true nature is forever on display, and how one can pretend otherwise is one of the world's great mysteries. It's available now, just as one is, and does not require the would-be seer to be holy, or virtuous, or learned, or clever, or special in any way. Rather the reverse. What a superb — and woefully neglected — advantage this is!

Second, this alone is real seeing, the only sort that's foolproof. Look and see now whether it's possible to perceive partially or dimly the emptiness where you are. This seeing of the subject — of the one who sees — is a perfect and all-or-nothing experience, in contrast to the seeing of objects, such as this page covered with black marks. A very great deal of the scene is missed, just not registered. In fact, the view out is never clear, the view in never foggy, as Shen-hui implies in the quotation that prefaces this chapter.

Third, this seeing goes deep. The clearest and "most distant" of the views out is found to be restricted and shallow — actually, it's paper-thin — in contrast to the view in, which visibly has no limits and goes on and on forever. It penetrates to the bottomless depths of our being, even to the Abyss from which all arises. No wonder it convinces as nothing else can convince, and leaves the seer in no doubt about its thoroughness. "There is no longer any need to believe," says the Sufi Al-Alawi, "when one sees the Truth."

Fourth, this experience, in spite of all its depth and mystery, is uniquely communicable, because it's exactly the same for all — for the Buddha, for Jesus, for Shen-hui, for Al-Alawi, for you and me. Inevitably so, seeing that this nothingness has nothing in it to differ about, nothing to go wrong, nothing idiosyncratic or merely personal and private. How unlike all those other experiences which are so hard — if not impossible — to share! However vividly you describe and try to demonstrate to me your thoughts and feelings and sensations, you can never be sure I'm getting the message. You and I agree to label the rose red, and sweet-scented, and charming, and so on, but the inner experience the label is attached to is essentially a private one, impossible to get across with any certainty to anyone else. What is for you red could be for me pink or orange, or even blue. But reverse the arrow of attention and all this uncertainty vanishes. Here and here alone, where all share a common nature, is perfect communication, everlasting agreement, no possibility of misunderstanding. This concord cannot be overrated, because it's the profoundest at-oneness about what we and all beings really, really are. And in the light of this basic assent we can afford to differ to any extent about what we and they seem to be, about appearances. Though the seer's relationship with others is transformed into identity with them, his humanness is likely to take a unique and unpredictable form. If ever there was a mixed bunch of people, the world's seers are among the most variegated.

Fifth and last, this seeing into nothingness is always on tap, whatever one's mood, whatever one is up to, no matter how calm or agitated one happens to be at the time. It's instantly available on demand, simply by looking in. This accessibility, when fully put to the test, may leave one's life outwardly the same, but inwardly it's revolutionized.

We have examined five inestimable virtues of this simple in-seeing, and found it to be easy, foolproof, deeper than deep, uniquely shareable, always to hand. But there's another side to this splendid picture, a variety of less welcome concomitants or snags, which we must now look at.

Some of these disadvantages arise from the very advantages of this in-seeing. For instance, just because it's so obvious, so available without notice and natural and ordinary, it's tragically easy to undervalue and dismiss offhand as quite trivial. Actually, in practice, its immense depth and spiritual power are nearly always overlooked, at least to begin with. How, it is argued, could so cheap a realization (in fact, it's scot-free) be worth much. Easy come, easy go. What moral discipline, what spiritual work have we put in, by which to earn any worthwhile spiritual gift? Then again, this least costly of realizations comes to us backed by no mystical credentials, endorsed by no burst of cosmic consciousness, no ecstasy. The bells of heaven aren't just muffled, they are pointedly silent. Here, in fact, is an all-time low rather than a high, a valley rather than one of those famous peak experiences. "It is a prosaic and nonglorious event ... Here is nothing painted in bright colors, all is gray and extremely unobtrusive and unattractive." Such are the sobering comments which one's initial seeing into nothingness are apt to excite, and with good reason. Our quotation is from D.T. Suzuki, the man who brought Zen to the West. He is describing *satori*, which is the Japanese term for seeing into nothingness, and he knew by experience what he was talking about. As for our earning this vision, or somehow traveling to the place where it's to be had, the idea is stuff and nonsense. And why? Why because *satori* is simply ceasing to turn a blind eye upon what we and all beings eternally are, upon what we are all living from anyway, regardless of merit, and aside from all mystical graces — or lack of them.

The truth is that such defects or snags — in particular the shallowness of the in-seeing — are no more than misunderstandings, readily cleared up as soon as we muster the courage to look for ourselves and take seriously what we find. The real snag is quite different, and on the face of it appears very serious. It is that the great majority of the people who are persuaded to look within and perceive briefly their true nature are happy to leave the experience at that. For them, apparently, it's little more than an intriguing adventure, an interesting way of looking at things — or maybe just good fun, a pleasant sort of children's game — and of no real importance for living. It's not for prolonging or repeating or testing, and certainly not for practicing. And so it has virtually no effect whatever, and seers remain in terribly short supply.

Well, what we can safely say about this last and truly formidable snag is something like this. All the great developments in human history have had very modest and virtually invisible beginnings. A tiny group of people fired with a truly revolutionary vision are in the long run far more powerful for change than all the dedicated adherents to some well-established cause or idea put together: and of all revolutions this turn around to what's nearer than near is by far the most revolutionary. I suspect that, something like a million years ago, it wasn't a boss proto-human who first tumbled to the hitherto unthinkable fact that out there in the water and in others' eyes, one has a face. My guess is that a solitary mother, gazing long at her reflection, got the point and, given a lot of luck, somehow managed to share it with one of her children. I suspect, further, that it was only after hundreds or thousands of years of touch-and-go that the idea began to take on at all. And now, of course, this kind of human self-consciousness is the norm to fall short of which is to be not yet fully human.

Don't tell me that the human saga has to end here and that our species has altogether run out of steam. Or that "the true seeing, the eternal seeing" has no chance of one day becoming the new norm for large numbers of the population, or even the majority.

Not that there's any likelihood of Utopia breaking out. Along with this new norm, if it is ever realized, will come new problems, some of which can already be foreseen. But at the very least it will show that this preposterous species of ours isn't irretrievably stuck in the mud of its prime delusion, namely, that one *is* here what one *looks like* over there. And that its self-awarded title of *sapiens* is not, after all, a prize example of black humor.

SELF-ENQUIRY: SOME OBJECTIONS ANSWERED

Our self-knowledge is our beauty; self-ignorant, we are ugly.
— PLOTINUS

All Christian religion consists wholly in this: to learn to know
ourselves, whence we come and what we are.
— BOEHME

Who is it that repeats the Buddha's name? We should try to
find out where this Who comes from and what it looks like.
— HSU YUN

You know the value of everything except yourself.
— RUMI

Forgetfulness of the Self is the source of all misery.
— RAMANA MAHARSHI

How is it that we need all this prodding, all these warnings and earnest invitations and promises of infinite rewards, to persuade us to take a really close look at ourselves? Why don't all intelligent and serious people make it their chief business in life to find out whose life it is?

Thoughtful people, when challenged on this delicate subject, are apt to excuse themselves by raising a number of objections to this inner search. They aren't at all sure it's a good thing. Of course all agree that we need a working knowledge of our nature in order to make the best use of ourselves and get on with others, but (they feel) the probing can thrust too deep and go on far too long. "Know thyself" is all right up to a point but shouldn't become an obsession, an end in itself, and certainly not our life's work. Introspection carried to such lengths is likely to do more harm than good.

Or, in more detail:

1. It's a selfish diversion of our energies from the service of others to preoccupation with ourselves.
2. It's a morbid introversion leading to excessive and handicapping self-consciousness (in the bad sense of that word) if not to mental illness.
3. It's time consuming and unpractical, unfitting us for our jobs and for family life.
4. It's depressing and a bore, leading (its practitioners themselves admit) to a dead end and mental blandness.
5. It kills spontaneity and all natural, outgoing enjoyment.
6. It's a wonderful excuse for idleness and sponging.
7. It's coldly indifferent to art and to Nature, to the beauty and wonder of the universe and the rich variety of the human scene.
8. It's a stupefying drug that kills creativity, reduces words to gibberish, stops thought, numbs the mind itself, exchanging our most highly evolved human functions for the nonhuman or subhuman Inane.

Let's explore these eight objections to Self-enquiry.

SELFISH?

We pay lip service to the dictum that we are not here to find ourselves but to forget ourselves, concentrating on others and exchanging our natural self-centeredness for the other-centeredness of loving service.

That's all very well, but how can we be sure we are doing others much good till we know ourselves? How much of our so-called help is working off our guilt feelings on the world, or indulging our craving for power, or white-washing some other grubby motive, regardless of the world's real need? How often our short-term help ends in long-term hindrance! It's notorious that the material and even the psychological aid we give people in solving one of their problems is apt to create two more. Only the kind of aid that's given by one who really knows himself, and others through himself, can be guaranteed altogether beneficent and free from those unfortunate side effects that go on and on so incalculably: and then the gift is probably a secret one, unexpressed and inexpressible. The truth is that helping oneself (which means finding oneself) *is* helping others, though the influence may be altogether subterranean. It goes without saying that we must be as actively kind as we can, but until we can see clearly Who is being kind we are working more or less in the dark, with the hit-or-miss consequences that might be expected.

Another trouble with this would-be forgetfulness of self in the service of others is that it's practically impossible anyway. Deliberate virtue rarely forgets to pat itself on the back a little. Goodness aimed at directly can scarcely avoid self-congratulation, and then it begins to smell less sweet. But if, on the other hand, it's a by-product, arising naturally out of true knowledge of oneself and concern for others because at root one *is* them, then it's indifferent to itself and any incidental merit earned, and continues to smell sweet. Unfortunately, trying to become a saint, or even a sage, is a self-defeating (or rather Self-defeating) enterprise likely to end in its opposite — an inflated ego.

MORBID?

Is there any truth in the opinion that radical Self-enquiry is sick?

What is mental illness, in the last resort, but alienation from others and therefore from oneself? It's the shame and misery of the part trying to become a whole (which it can never be) instead of the Whole (which it always is). We are all more or less ill till we find by Self-enquiry our Oneness with everyone else.

UNPRACTICAL?

Self-enquiry is also suspected of being, if not actually sick, at least unbalanced and abnormal, unfitting us for life. Some color is given to this objection by the fact (painfully evident to anyone who gets mixed up with religious movements) that "spiritual" people are quite often cranks, misfits, or inclined to be neurotic. Actually this isn't surprising. Contented (not to say self-satisfied) people, fairly "normal" and halfway good at being human, aren't driven to finding out what else they may be, their divinity. It's those who need to find out Who they are, the fortunately desperate ones, who are more likely to go in for Self-discovery. A sound instinct tells them where their cure lies.

So it is that initially the worldling may appear to be, and often is, a far better person than the spiritually inclined, and certainly looking within doesn't transform the personality overnight. All the same, to the degree that this supreme enterprise succeeds, it "normalizes" a man, fitting him at last for life and correcting awkwardnesses and weaknesses and uglinesses. Now he's truly adjusted; he knows how to be at peace. Paradoxically, it's by discovering that he isn't a man at all that he becomes a satisfactory man. Once he steadily sees into his Nature his needs and his demands on others rapidly dwindle, his ability to concentrate on any chosen task is remarkable, his detachment provides the cool objectivity necessary for practical wisdom. For the first time he sees people for what they are really worth, he takes in everything but is himself not taken in. At the start Self-enquiry may not be the best recipe for making friends and influencing people, but in the end it's the only way to be at home in the world. Nothing else is quite practical. Sages are immensely effectual people, not a lot of dreamy incompetents.

DULL?

Ah (say those who don't know) but their life is so uninteresting, so monotonous. How is it possible — attending for months and years on end to what is admittedly featureless, without any content whatever, mere Clarity — to avoid a terrible boredom? Discovering our North Pole may be fine, but do we have to live there in the icy wasteland where nothing ever happens?

Now the extraordinary truth is that, contrary to all expectations, this seemingly bleak and dreary Center of our being is in fact endlessly fascinating: there's not a dull moment here. It's our periphery, the world where things happen, which in the end bores and depresses. Why should the colorless, unchanging, shapeless, empty, nameless Source (in actual practice, not in theory) prove forever fresh and charming, while all its products, in spite of their inexhaustible richness, sooner or later prove a great weariness? Well, this happy fact, plus the happy fact that our vision of the source is always available, just has to be accepted — thankfully. It can hardly be a matter of serious complaint that everything lets us down till we see "who" never lets us down.

Unnatural?

Everything naturally directs us back to its Source within us. In fact, the whole business of Self-discovery is our normal function, our natural development and growing up, failing which we remain stunted, if not perverse or freakish. Again, this is a surprising discovery. One would have imagined that any protracted inward gaze would have made a man rather less natural, probably giving him a withdrawn look, an odd and self-occupied and forbidding manner. Actually the reverse is true. The Self-seeing man has the grace and the charm of one who is free. To find the source is to tap it.

Take the case of one who is morbidly self-conscious. There are two things he can do about it, the one an amelioration (if that), the other a true cure. The false remedy for his shyness is to lose himself by moving outwards towards the world, the true remedy is to find himself by moving inwards towards himself, till one day his self-consciousness is replaced by Self-consciousness and he is at ease everywhere. It's true, of course, that nobody can, by any technique of self-forgetting, regain the simple openness of the small child and the animal. Nevertheless by the opposite technique of Self-recollection he can regain something like that blessed state, at a much higher level. Then he will know, not by taking thought but by a kind of immediate instinct, what to do and how to do it. And, rather more often perhaps, what not to do. Short of this goal, we are all to some degree awkward and artificial and putting on some act or other.

Idle?

Is this a soft option, an easy way out of the Hell of responsibility and involvement and danger into a safe and unstrenuous Heaven? Not so. In a sense, admittedly, it's the easiest thing in the world to see what nobody else can see, namely what it's like to be oneself right here at no distance from oneself: the Emptiness is blazingly obvious, the Clarity absolutely transparent and unmistakable. But in another sense, alas, it's the most difficult thing in the world to see and go on seeing this Spot from this spot. The trouble is that this mysterious Place one occupies, where one supposed there was some solid thing and in fact is only the Seer Himself, is *too* wide open to inspection, *too* obvious and *too* plain to capture our attention. All our arrows of attention point outwards, and they might be made of steel, so seemingly hard it is to bend them round to point in at the Center, and still harder to prevent them springing back again immediately. Of all ambitions this is the most far-reaching, and no other adventure is anything like so daring and "difficult" — till we see how the "difficulty" was a nonsense of our own making.

WORLD-REJECTING?

Is the game of Self-enquiry worth the candle? The answer is surely "no" if there's nothing of value out there, nothing worthy of our dedicated attention and love. Turning our backs on a universe so teeming and so magnificent, on all the treasures of art and of thought, and above all on our fellow humans, is surely a huge loss. Yet the sage — so it's reported — isn't interested in these matters: the world consists of things he doesn't wish to know. For him (they say) knowledge of particular things is ignorance.

The facts are the other way round. Oddly enough, it's the man who attends only to the outer scene, ignoring what lies at its Center, who is more or less blind to that scene. For the world is a curious phenomenon that, like a faint star, can be clearly observed only when it isn't directly looked at. The world will hide its true face from us until we look in the opposite direction, catching sight of it in the mirror of the Self.

For example, though the world is occasionally beautiful in places when directly viewed as quite real and self-supporting, it's consistently beautiful when indirectly viewed as an overflowing of the Self. When you see "Who's" really here you see what's really there, as a sort of bonus. This bonus comes as surprise on surprise. The universe is transformed. Colors sing they are so brilliant and glowing, shapes and planes and textures arrange themselves into charming compositions, nothing's repulsive or ugly or out of place. Every random patterning of objects — treetops and cloud banks, leaves and stones littering the ground, reflections in shop windows, stains and the tattered remains of posters on old walls, rubbish of all kinds — each is seen to be inevitable and perfect in its own unique way. And this is the very opposite of human imagination. It's divine realism, the clearing of that imaginative and wordy smokescreen which increasingly hides the world from us as we grow older and more knowing.

UNCREATIVE?

The path of Self-enquiry is indeed no escape route. It's the short way in to the universe as it is, our highboard to immersion in the world. Yet, they say, it's incompatible with any other serious creative endeavor, whether artistic or intellectual or practical. If this is so, then here is surely a considerable drawback.

It's true that Self-enquiry will never succeed till we put our whole heart into it, and consequently the dedicated artist or philosopher or scientist would seem to be an unpromising candidate for sagehood. If so, this is not because he's too devoted to his calling but not devoted enough, not yet absolutely serious about it. He needs to deepen and widen his field till it includes both himself and the whole world. For the only consistent genius, the only complete artist-philosopher-scientist is the sage who is fully conscious of being the Painter of the world picture, the Thinker of all thought, the Universe-inventor, Knowledge itself. This doesn't mean, of course, that he has all the details at his fingertips, but he does see what they all amount to in their innermost essence and outermost sum. Namely, his true Self. And when a question of detail arises his response is the right one. His mindlessness is the indispensable basis of a smoothly functioning mind. His Self-knowledge contains all the information he needs from moment to moment. In short, the sage is *sage*, not clever and learned and with a head full of ideas but truly simple and clearheaded. Precisely so.

Even in ordinary life we find hints of this vital connection between Self-awareness and creativity. Don't our very best moments always include a heightened consciousness of ourselves, so that we aren't really lost in inspiration or creative fervor or love, but newly found? At its finest, doesn't the opaque object over there point unmistakably back to the transparent Subject here? It may even happen that the transparency comes first: we attend, our idiotic chatter dies down, we consciously become nothing but this alert, expectant Void — and presently the required tune or picture, the key notion, the true answer, arise ready-made in that Void, from that Void.

The result of observing only the universe is anxiety. Only observing the Observer of the universe will put a stop to a man's worrying and fussing and scheming. When his interest is diverted inwards he naturally relaxes his hold — his stranglehold — on the outer world. Having withdrawn his capital and paid it into his own Central Bank (where it appreciates to infinity), he has nothing to lose out there and no reason for interfering. He knows how to let things be and work out in their own time. He's in no hurry. Knowing the Self, he can hardly fail to trust its products. Whatever occurs is fundamentally agreeable to him. In Christian terms, he has no will but God's: what he wants is what happens and what happens is what he wants. Paradoxically his obedience to the nature of things is his rule over them. His weakness is in the long run all-powerful. And the secret of his power over things is that he goes to the Source. "Seek ye first the Kingdom of God, and all these things shall be added unto you." Seek ye first these things, and even they shall be taken away.

This perfect obedience isn't just lining oneself up with God's will, or imitating it, or even becoming part of it. It's that very will itself in full operation. If we wish to find out what it's really like to create the world, we have only to desire nothing and pay attention. But total acceptance is very hard. It's precisely the opposite of the lazy indifference that lets things slide. It springs from inner strength and not weakness, from concentration, not slackness. Why is the world so troublesome, so frightful? Is it like that by nature, or because we take the easy way of fighting it instead of the difficult way of fitting in with it? We have to find out for ourselves the truth of the sage's demonstration that even in the smallest things the way of noninterference, of giving up all self-will, of "disappearing," is astonishingly practical, the way that works. Not only in the long run but from moment to moment consciously getting out of the Light, giving place to whatever happens to be presenting itself in that Light, is astonishingly creative. We do too much and therefore remain ineffectual, we talk far too much and therefore say nothing, we think far, far too much and therefore prevent the facts from speaking for themselves — so say those who know the value of emptiness. It's for us to make our own tests, not — repeat *not* — by the direct method of trying to be quiet and mindless (it just won't work) but by the indirect method of seeing Who, it seems, was trying to be like that. No man becomes Godlike except by seeing that he isn't a man anyway.

His experience of deification has no content whatsoever, no details. It's not merely indescribable but nonmental and nonpsychological and in the truest sense nonhuman. Thinking or talking about it kills it by complicating what is Simplicity and Obviousness itself. It's rather like tasting sugar or seeing green: the more you reflect on it the further you get from the actuality. But there the resemblance ends. Seeing green is an ineffable experience because it's a prehuman or infrahuman one; seeing the Seer of green is an ineffable experience because it's a posthuman or suprahuman one. The sage's rejection of the concept-ridden, word-clouded mind isn't retrogression but the next evolutionary step beyond man, or rather the whole path from him to the goal of Self-realization. And though that goal is beyond thought, pure limpidity, void even of voidness, it's nothing but the Honest Truth at last. For only the Self can be known: everything else is partly guess-work, partly false, not all there. Only Self-awareness is wide-awake and fully observant: all other awareness is a kind of mind-wandering. Total awareness *is* the Self.

And so, in conclusion, every fault we could find with Self-enquiry has turned out to be a merit, thinly disguised. Certainly there are kinds of introspection which are harmful, but they are concerned with the ego or empirical self and the very opposite of the true enquiry which is healthy and sane, creative, natural, life-enhancing, practical, and al-truistic. Though some of us may start this true enquiry terribly late, it's what we are here for. To neglect it is in every sense a shame.

It would still be a shameful neglect and cop-out, unworthy of our energy and intelligence, even if our Self-enquiry came up with no pay-off at all. In any case its benefits, though immense, are not the point. The only way to have them is not to go for them but only for the unvarnished Truth about ourselves, no matter how unedifying it might turn out to be. If all we want is to see Who we really, really are, nothing can stop us from doing so this very moment. But if our plan is to use that blessed vision to buy baskets full of nice feelings or any other goodies, we might as well abandon the very idea of Self-enquiry.

THE VARIETIES
OF MYSTICAL
EXPERIENCE

Self-realization, according to Ramana Maharshi, "is really like gazing into vacancy", into an emptiness in which even "the thought 'I am Brahman' has to vanish."

This raises the whole question of the nature of Self-realization, of how the true spiritual life is lived, of what mystical experience is all about. If that experience is as barren as these quotations from an expert declare, then what price those marvelous utterances of the great mystics, East and West, ancient and modern, which describe not emptiness but a glorious fullness, the enjoyment of all sorts of spiritual riches, insights, revelations?

What *is* mysticism? Of all the loaded words we use and misuse this is one of the most ambiguous, and also among those we can least afford to be vague about. What *do* we mean by mystical experience? What are the marks of the true mystic?

Anyone naive enough to set out answering these questions by paying a visit to a bookshop and dipping into the books on the "mystical" shelves would invite total confusion. What connection could he find between clairvoyance and the Godhead of Meister Eckhart, between colorful stories of miracles and the Void that is void even of voidness, between dowsing and the stigmata of Padre Pio, between astral travel and out-of-the-body experiences and the claim by some mystics that they were never in the body anyhow? How could any sensible person bracket those mystics who describe the essential awareness as enjoyment of this or that state or quality or idea — such as love, joy, freedom, aliveness — with those mystics who insist that the essential aware-ness has no content at all, is clean of all thinking and feeling?

Let's try to clear up this mass of confusion by sharply distinguish-ing three kinds of experience which, though commonly lumped to-gether under the heading *mystical*, are in fact about as different as they could be.

1. The first sort need not keep us long. Here mystical means mysteri-ous, odd, inexplicable, occult, weird, beyond belief, unnatural, in-compatible with science. I remember buying many years ago, on the strength of its title, a book called *The Mystical Life*. It turned out to be an account of the author's journeys in a state of trance, through astronomical regions unknown to science, and the strong implica-tion was that here we had the very stuff of mystical experience and that no other sort deserved to be taken very seriously. In fact, this variety of mysticism covers a huge field, from flying saucers and numerology to the strange worlds of Emmanuel Swedenborg and Rudolph Steiner and William Butler Yeats. This isn't to deny all value and significance to this kind of experience (there's always *something* in it — look at Yeats' best poetry) but to point out how different it is from mystical experience of the second sort.

2. Rather than trying to describe this variety, let's take an example. In his well-known and pioneering treatise, significantly entitled *Cosmic Consciousness: A Study in the Evolution of the Human Mind*, Dr. R.M. Bucke wrote:

    There came upon me a state of exultation, of immense joyousness, accompanied or immediately followed by an intellectual illumination quite impossible to de-scribe. Among other things, I did not merely come to believe, I saw that the universe is not composed of dead matter but is, on the contrary, a living Presence; I became conscious in myself of eternal life. It was not a conviction that I would have eternal life, but a con-sciousness that I possessed eternal life then; I saw that all men are immortal; that the cosmic order is such that beyond any peradventure all things work together for the good of each and all; that the foundation prin-ciple of the world, of all the worlds, is what we call love, and that the happiness of each and all is certain. The vision lasted a few seconds and was gone. But the

memory of it has remained during the quarter of a
century that has since elapsed. I knew that what the
vision showed was true.

This second variety of mystical experience is at least as concerned with the truth of what's being experienced as with the ac-
companying thrills and delights. It claims to arrive at self-evident
Facts of immense importance, hitherto concealed. It comes as
knowledge of a higher and happier order, and conversely as the
discovery of underlying Realities. It is a revelation or a series of
revelations. An example is the strong sense of sharing in the peace
and love and joy and other wonderful things that are to be found
in our Source, at the very heart of all beings. Here is a diamond
with innumerable facets, many-colored, fiery-brilliant, irradiating
the world.

The experience we are examining, though so varied as to baffle
definition, does have four distinct marks. *First*, it cannot be had at
will, laid on to order. You can do little or nothing to bring it on.
Amazing grace rarely responds to urgent invitations. *Second*, it cannot free itself from its thought-content and feeling-content. Love
is not the same as joy or peace or compassion or courage. And, of
course, specific experiences like this, no matter how exalted, are
necessarily limited and partial. None covers the whole field of the
Real. *Third*, it has a certain vagueness and cannot be pinned down
for inspection. It spills over. No wonder this variety of mystical
experience can be remembered only as a pale ghost of itself. In
any case it is a matter of degree. Mystical experiences vary in in-
tensity from moment to moment, and (it's safe to say) from mystic
to mystic. Some are very gifted, others less so. There's a hierarchy
of spiritual attainment. *Fourth* and last, it is temporal. It's in time
and it takes time. It comes out of the blue, flourishes (as Bucke
says) briefly, and goes, perhaps never to return. And certainly never
to return in precisely that form. It's the rarest and swiftest of birds
that has never been observed sitting.

3. Now these four characteristics — unpredictability, incompleteness
    or partiality, vagueness and brevity — which are the marks of our
    second variety of mystical experience, do not apply to our third
    kind at all. In most respects, in fact, it is the opposite of the sort of
    thing we have been looking at so far. If we call, for convenience,

our first variety Popular Mysticism and our second Peak-experi-
ence Mysticism, and this third variety Liberated Mysticism, then it
is indeed a mysticism that is liberated from the shortcomings of
mysticism — and, truly speaking, from mysticism itself. Thus:

Firstly, this experience is accessible, at will, whatever my mood or
state of health or merits or demerits. All I need to do to see into my
Essential Nature is to turn round the arrow of my attention at this very
moment and see that I am looking at this word processor out of nothing whatever, and certainly not out of a small, opaque, colored, complicated thing. The spot I occupy right now is awake to the fact that it
is, on present evidence, not occupied by me but by a word processor. I
am Aware Space for that machine to happen in. And if I should doubt
this I have only to point at my "face" and notice what's on my side of
that pointing finger.

Secondly, this experience is a mind-stopper. What I find here has
no perceptual content, no feeling content, no thought content. I like
to call it a kind of alert idiocy, free from ideas and emotions of any
sort, and certainly of the mystical sort. This doesn't mean I'm in any
sort of trance, or that there is anything odd or unnatural about this
state. Quite the contrary: it is ceasing to pretend that I am what I'm
not, a thing in the world, a minded thing. It isn't that I deny or reject
the contents of my awareness but that I awaken to the fact that where I
am is stainless Clarity, free from all qualities or contents or functions.
The mind cannot penetrate this depth, to the true Valley Experience.

Thirdly, this vision of the deepest Deep has nothing vague about it.
It is precision itself. It cannot be doubted. It is self-evident, clear, simple,
all-or-nothing, and there's no way to get it wrong. There are no inferior sightings of "who" one really is. You can go on forever getting
more beautiful feelings, more brilliant thoughts, more profound insights, but when you come home to their Origin there is only one way
of being there. What you see is perfectly seen, as it is, for ever and ever.

Fourthly, this experience is out of time. It is only now. That is why it
can never be remembered or anticipated, but only enjoyed in the
present moment. And when so enjoyed no date or hour can be attributed to it. "I saw "who" I was from 3:00 p.m. to 4:35 p.m." makes no
sense at all. This isn't for discussing but for testing. Examine now the
Absence that lies at the center of your universe, and you will notice
that your inspection has no beginning or ending. The experience ac-

tually reads as timeless.

In practically every respect, then, our third type of mystical experience is sharply contrasted with the others, and we have no excuse for confusing it with them. To get rid of this confusion is to get rid of one of the basic problems of the spiritual life.

Let me cite an instance of this problem-solving. Friends who really do turn their attention round and perceive their Source commonly complain that it does nothing for them, that they remain all-too-human, petty, moody, the mixture as before. Or they are deeply disappointed to find that this in-seeing isn't a mystical experience at all in the accepted meaning of that expression, and certainly can't be counted on to produce high-grade thoughts or feelings. The mistake such friends are making, of course, is to mix up Variety (2) with Variety (3), Peak Experiences with the Valley Experience which is truly liberating. I suggest that their best hope of getting their full share of Peak Experiences is not to go after them directly (a fruitless pursuit) but to rest in their Source. And then I suspect that the Source will, in spite of its absolute plainness (in both senses of that word) grow on them to such an extent that they will lose interest in Peak Experiences, and in the mind itself with its ever-changing weather, so that what finally fascinates is the Space it all happens in.

To sum up, then, our first type of mystic is fascinated by the *strange* things that come and go in that Space, our second type by the best things (the most true and good and beautiful things) that come and go in that Space, our third type by the Space itself, the Aware Space which includes and transcends all concepts — including that of Aware Space!

Not that I'm keen on labeling this third variety *mysticism* at all. In fact you could call it *anti-mysticism* and certainly *anti-mystification*, or just being attentive and natural and what one so obviously is for oneself: no longer out-for-lunch but in-for-lunch, and enjoying a hearty appetite.

THE
LAST
UPANISHAD?

Lead me from dreaming to waking.
Lead me from opacity to clarity.
Lead me from the complicated to the simple.
Lead me from the obscure to the obvious.
Lead me from intention to attention.
Lead me from what I'm told I am to what I see I am.
Lead me from confrontation to wide openness.
Lead me to the place I never left,
Where there is peace, and peace, and peace.
—THE UPANISHADS

His former creation having ended in chaos, the Lord of the Universe was considering the next one. So He called in the gods to advise Him about the new venture. They expressed delight for they saw an opportunity to remedy a defect the last universe had suffered from: namely, that He had remained on high in a state of deep meditation, far from His creatures. The consequences of this remoteness, they reminded Him, were disastrous.

"This time," they humbly insisted, "we beg You to be more accessible. For even the best ideas and feelings *about You* are no substitute whatsoever for *You*, and are a million leagues adrift from Your awesome Presence. The people need to see You. Hearsay is almost no use at all."

"I understand the problem perfectly," He graciously conceded. "This time I shall get right into My world. Moreover I shall drop all disguises and make Myself perfectly obvious. Wherever people are gathered together I shall be there among them, plainer than plain. I promise there will be a sure and easy — indeed startling — way of recognizing Me."

"And what will that be?" they inquired eagerly.

"I shall turn Myself into a Cyclops, an Oddity — you could say a Monster — with a single eye. All those folks around Me peeking and peering out of a pair of tiny peepholes apiece, and Me gazing steadily and clear-eyed out of one immense, wide-open, staring Optic, far bigger than the body it's mounted on! Why I shall stand out so prominently it will be quite embarrassing!"

The Lord of the Universe made good His promise. Taking on this striking and unique form, He turned up in His new universe. Of every group the truly wide-eyed Lord of the Universe was a member.

And nobody noticed Him! Incredibly, people went on overlooking the Divine Oddity in their midst.

His counselors, shocked and bewildered, could hardly believe it. They said to Him, "See how perverse, how blind, how crazy these people are! You will have to remodel Yourself even more drastically if You are to stand a chance of waking them up and attracting their attention."

The Lord was so shocked, so outraged that He drew His great sword and in one blow cut His own head clean off, single eye and all.

"As this beheaded but (please note) still very much alive trunk," He exclaimed, "how could I fail to stand out among all those headed creatures? Besides, as this unique One Who sees where there are no eyes, and hears where there are no ears, and smells where there is no nose, and tastes where there is no tongue, why I shall be the Wonder of the ages, of all ages! What's more, as the Headless One Who is wide open to all the heads in the world — as the One Who, having nothing to keep them out with, disappears in their favor — I shall proclaim to heaven and earth the end of the curse of Confrontation, of the mortal sickness that has plagued them from the beginning."

The gods were full of admiration and gratitude for this divine revelation to end all revelations.

But no! Hard as it is to believe, the only people who noticed and dared to point out their truncated Lord were some children who were either laughed at or ticked off, and a sprinkling of grown-ups who were either written off or polished off.

The gods were astounded and desperate. All they could do was advise their Lord to transmogrify Himself still more drastically, if that were possible, in the forlorn hope of attracting attention.

Again, though hurt and amazed, He agreed. After careful thought He settled on the following emergency measures, piling evidence upon evidence of His holy Presence.

"For a start, I shall turn Myself upside-down. You notice how people wear their heads on top, their bodies lower down, their feet at the bottom of the picture. Well, I shall wear My body the other way up. My feet will go to the top, followed by My legs, My thighs, My belly and chest. How will they manage to blind themselves to such a contrast?

"Not for My own sake but for theirs, I shall insist on VIP treatment always and everywhere. Here are four examples. When I stand on the seashore the carpet of golden light will unroll itself between the rising or setting sun and Me alone: never will it lead up to one of My creatures. All vertical lines, such as the corners of the room I happen to be in, will pay homage to My Presence by visibly inclining towards Me. My body will always bulk much larger than the bodies of the people around Me, rather as the king in their early paintings bulked much larger than mere courtiers and servants. Above all, I shall invariably station Myself at the center of the universe and let nobody push Me to one side.

"Alone in all the changing scene I shall stay rock-steady and immovable. No matter how active these legs, I shall be the Stillness in which they and all things move. Whereas others go down an aisle or avenue or corridor, it will go down Me. When I mount My chariot, it will be to make the roadside trees and houses and hedges rush by, to drive My world. I shall never bother to go anywhere but instead sit quite still and bring places and things to me, and send them away when I have done with them.

"Regardless of all this divine showmanship, of all My desperate attempts to get through to these blockheads, I shall remain in the place where no time, no change, not even the smell of death can enter, in the one and only timeless region. While everywhere else has its calendars and timepieces, none will survive in the place I occupy. Any watch or clock approaching Me I shall magically cause to swell and burst and disappear without trace. I solemnly promise that, in whatever room people happen to meet, there will be one spot on the floor which visibly stops and destroys all timepieces. To find it will be to find Me, the deathless One, the Eternal."

"Enough, O Lord!" cried His counselors. "Your Self-revelation has exceeded all we could have imagined or hoped for. More than this your creatures could hardly bear. Almost too numerous, too dazzling, too inescapable are the promised evidences of Your sacred Presence among them."

"Quite so," replied their Lord. "But for good measure let Me flaunt My divine powers to the limit, and mercilessly show up the feebleness of the people around Me. They will not be able to avoid seeing Me change, and destroy, and recreate the world at will and all the time. Nor will they be able to avoid seeing that — whether they look up or down or rotate or shut and open their little eyes — nothing happens to the world. It ignores them, of course. It's My world, and I'll show them Who is in control.

"Well, my esteemed panel of advisors," He concluded, "how will that do?"

"Such a Divine Marvel in their midst," they replied, "such a Compendium of Wonders, how could You pass unnoticed for a moment?"

But it was not to be! Astonishingly, almost no one noticed Him. In spite of such a superabundance of clues, He remained incognito, lost in the crowd. What irony! The Origin of the World found Himself cut and blackballed and sent to Coventry by His world, the victim or mark of an elaborate conspiracy to get rid of Him by systematically ignoring or pooh-poohing every trace of His existence as it cropped up. The ultimate Snub, you could call it, or Theocide by a Thousand Cuts.

A meeting of the gods was called to deal with the crisis. After long consideration, they addressed their Lord:

"These folk are deliberately blind to the obvious and their own welfare. Indeed it seems that the more striking Your distinguishing marks, the less they register. So we humbly suggest that You should try a very different strategy. Instead of the demonstrative approach — or rather, in addition to it — in addition to trying to impress them with the power and the glory of Your Presence among them, why not try intimacy? What they stubbornly refuse to see they may at last be led to feel. Come close to them. Appeal to their hearts."

As ever, He obliged.

"Very well. From now on I shall stand aloof from no one. While all those creatures around Me keep their distance from one another —

each cold-shouldering the rest — I shall stay distant from none. Even the longest measuring rod, held up between Me and them, I shall shrink to nothing, to a point. Thus I shall draw everyone to Me, irresistibly, in the love affair of all time.

"More than this, much more than this, I shall give My very life for them. Let Me explain. All around I see those headed ones engaged in what they call personal relationships, each visibly ranged against and opposed to his or her opposite number, face to face in head-on collision. As a particular thing each excludes every other particular thing. To be and to remain itself, each insists on its unique and separate identity vis-a-vis the rest. That is their attitude, their posture, as they shape up for conflict. But I shall manifest a quite different shape, another posture altogether."

"And what will that be?" His counselors inquired.

"In fact," He replied, "it is done. Already I'm built wide, wide open, built for harmony and peace and love. It is plain that for Me and Me alone, for this drastically Truncated One, there can be no head-on collisions, no confrontations, in a sense no relationships of any sort, but only perfect union with all comers. Face there to no-face here, I give place to them, I disappear so that they may appear. I die continually as Myself so that they may come alive in Me. Thus forever giving My life for the world I would seek to win all hearts."

The gods were deeply moved.

"This time it will be hard indeed to ignore You, Lord. Just think of the accumulated wealth of clues to Your Presence, the abundance of Your distinguishing marks. Who could fail to pick out the single-eyed, truncated, up-side down One Who makes and unmakes His world instantly and at will, Who destroys time and timepieces and folds space like an umbrella — and now the One Who, in spite of this matchless splendor, humbly prefers and makes way for the humblest of His creatures?"

And did these quite extraordinary measures work? No! Not on your life! Still the Lord of the Universe in their midst passed unnoticed, except by the very few.

The gods were very angry. "And the crowning irony of it all," they expostulated to their Lord, "is that large numbers of these people go on worshipping You with prayers and hymns that accurately describe You, and even go so far as to say where You may be found, which is right among them, nearer than near. What sort of devotees are these who are careful not to seek You in the one place where You are certainly to be found, brilliantly on show? Who will not or dare not see You Who are more obvious than Obvious?"

"Well," He asked, "is this the end? Is it back to the cosmic drawing board, and a brave new world replacing this cowardly crazy one?"

Taking counsel among themselves, the gods decided that no further pointers to their Lord would make any appreciable difference. They realized that whereas *any one* of these clues (from His single eye to His unceasing Self-giving) is enough to locate Him with perfect ease — if that's what one wants to do — *all* of those clues together aren't enough to locate Him — if that's what one is determined *not* to do. Such willful blindness to Him will never be cured by multiplying and floodlighting His distinguishing features. Most reluctantly they concluded that only desperate need stood a chance of opening these people's eyes to the Presence among them of the One Who alone can meet that need. If the choice became inescapable — SEE HIM OR PERISH! — why, then at last He might suddenly stand out in all His obviousness and majesty and saving power.

So His counselors said to Him, "We are agreed that this latest design of Yours for a world has gone all wrong, and that the time is drawing near when You should wipe the slate clean and start all over again. However there remains just one last hope for these creatures. Up to now they have been spared the full consequences of their willful blindness. The time has come to reveal the horror of those consequences. Allow them to discover the means of self-destruction, of genocide, and see whether fear — if not plain horse sense — will do what all else has failed to do. There's just a chance that their likely fate will at last bring them to their senses (repeat *to their senses*) to the One they can't help seeing but refuse to see. To the One Who never confronted anyone, to the One Who is the only remedy for confrontation and the mass suicide it must lead to."

"And what are the chances," the Lord interposed, "of their recognizing Me in time to avert disaster?" The tone of His voice was skeptical.

"If it had to be all of them," they replied, "then we grant that the chances are nil. However, a quite small but influential minority — not so much wielders of power as leaders of opinion — awakened to Your Presence, could perhaps set a trend; so that to enjoy You, O Lord, would become the norm, the accepted standard of maturity — attained by the few, recognized (however dimly) by the many. Rather as the beautiful ideal of sainthood used to be acknowledged and revered by the masses, who had no intention whatsoever of attempting anything of the kind. Thus at the 11th hour and 59th minute genocide might be avoided."

"Well perhaps," replied the Lord, not committing Himself. "But what exactly do you want Me to do?"

After a long debate His advisors came up with the following recommendations:

"*First*, we confirm that You should indeed let these people develop their science — pure, applied and grievously misapplied — to such a pitch that they are in danger of wiping themselves out. But, *second*, grant them the wit to extend their pure science of objects to include You Who are Purity itself and the Subject of all objects. In other words, let them bring to the study of You, O Lord, the same rigor and discipline, the same humility in front of the evidence which they have so successfully (and so disastrously) brought to Your creation; and let them go on to investigate in detail the many evidences of Your Presence among them, and the many ways in which You measurably (and photographically) differ so strikingly from them. Third, let them develop means of communication capable of disseminating this ultimate and divine science on such a scale and so speedily that their self-destruction, through ignorance of You, may at the last minute be averted. Graciously grant these gifts, O Lord, and let us see what they do with them."

"I am already in the process of granting all three," He replied. "And while we await the outcome, just a word of encouragement to anyone who, though clearly seeing Me, is daunted by the seemingly impossible task of getting the world to start doing so. Here numbers cloud the issue and the rules of arithmetic do not apply. When one of My creatures finds Me, just *who* finds Me? Is it that one as his or her private and solitary self, or as all other selves too, or as the Self that is Myself?

"Look and see."

THE NEAR END: THE SCIENCE OF LIBERATION AND THE LIBERATION OF SCIENCE

Science goes deeply into things. But not deeply enough — as yet. Far below the mind and what's left of matter there's a depth which, though pivotal and perfectly accessible, remains overlooked and unexplored. You and I together — in the next half hour — shall turn the searchlight of science onto those deepest foundations which till now have been hidden from all but the great contemplatives. Rare and gifted souls who, nevertheless, lacking the method and tools and language of science, were unable to present their discoveries as the readily verifiable facts they are. The result is that this fundamental level of our Nature is abandoned to superstitious fears and the most deadly of false assumptions. Not the sort of base on which to build a beautiful life!

The need for sound foundations is obvious. Defects in them soon become all too evident in the superstructure. We live above ground in the light, of course, but the quality and the safety of the life we live there rests upon what's below ground in the dark. The gigantic superstructure of our life is falling apart because so much of it is built on quicksand — on unexamined quicksand, at that. In plain language, it's the basic assumptions that you and I make about ourselves and our status in the world — and hence about the world itself — that are the trouble.

They boil down to one universal but well-hidden assumption: *I am what I look like.* These six little words are big enough to cover the whole reason for our plight. They say it all. Or, to elaborate somewhat: *I am here, for myself, what I look like over there, to you* — as if our distance made no difference! On this morass you and I try to build our lives. No wonder they are cracking up. To render them safe and sound we must rebuild them on the bedrock of *I am what I see I am here; what you see is just one of my regional appearances*. I alone, at center, am in a position to say what those myriad appearances are appearances of, and how different they *all* are from the one Reality that's giving rise to them, from what I'm looking out of. On this I'm the sole and final authority. I have inside information denied to all outsiders.

The question we're addressing isn't what you and I happen to feel or understand about ourselves — which is largely what the world currently happens to feel and understand — but what we see clearly once we dare to look. Our feelings and thoughts are the ever-changing mists that swirl above the rock of what we really are. To build on them is one worse than building on sand. It's building castles in the air, which, however impressive, are uninhabitable.

I'm inviting you to doubt what the world tells you about your identity, and take a fresh look at yourself for yourself. Just as I'm the sole and final authority on what I am for me at center, so are you the sole and final authority on what you are for you at center, in your own firsthand experience right now, when you drop all presuppositions and are true to yourself.

That's to say, when you approach our subject — which is *the* Subject, yourself as First Person — in a thoroughly scientific fashion.

The method of science has six main ingredients, the proportions varying from case to case:

1. *A hypothesis*, a theory or hunch, which may be about practically anything at all, so long as it can be stated clearly and tested by experiment and refined and developed. And that includes the age-old proposition which you are presently going to verify the truth of — the breathtaking proposition that you are the very opposite of the puny, restless and ephemeral thing you seem to be when viewed from out there.

2. *A challenge* to prevailing assumptions — less politely, superstitions. Daring to doubt and defy Authority and even indulge in fun at its expense.

3. *Apparatus or instruments* for sharpening one's senses and making the testing process more rigorous.

4. *Observation* or *looking to see*. That is to say: reliance on what you perceive instead of what you conceive, on active trial and error

instead of idle and wordy speculation. Going by what's present for you now, instead of what belongs to other persons and places and times. Counting on what you can count and quantify, which includes 0 and X, zero and infinity, as well as all between.

5. *Predicting the consequences* which should follow from your theory. For instance, the return of Haley's Comet in 2060, or what you may expect to find when, reversing your attention, you observe the observer of Haley's Comet.

6. *A formulation and sharing of your discoveries,* for verification by others. Invite selected friends to repeat the experiments and compare their findings with yours.

I'm not only asking you to carry out our tests or experiments along these six guidelines, but also fixing you up with the necessary apparatus — so there's no excuse for postponing them. Except, of course, our immense resistance to the Given, the Obvious, the Simple, as soon as they challenge the basic assumptions we live by. Just reading about these experiments (telling yourself you know what you would see) is to miss their point and side with the forces of superstition. And if at first they seem weird, not to say silly, it's no wonder. This new field of scientific enquiry needs new tools for its cultivation. For ages, of course, dedicated seers have been looking into what it is to BE AT CENTER, but this is the first application of the sixfold scientific method to that most fundamental of research projects. The first time that the science of the object has included the scientist himself as Subject eagerly and from the beginning instead of reluctantly, when forced by the facts to start taking him into account. *Already the result of this extension of science is that the clear vision of our essential Nature (to see it at all is to see it as it is) can be had at will and shared at once and for sure with anyone who's interested.* For instance, with you, in the next few minutes.

TEST 1. COUNTING EYES

It's not that the world *tells* you that you are peering at it through two tiny peepholes in a superior kind of meatball. It doesn't need to. Nobody doubts it. Of all obvious things this is the most obvious! Or is it?

For this experiment you need a scientific instrument called an eye-opener, which you make up with your fingers, like this [top drawing on following page]:

Out there are two framed pictures, two windows, each about 4 centimeters. But your seeing goes on nearer home. So, very slowly and attentively put your eye-opener right on, like a pair of frilly spectacles, watching what happens to those windows as you do so. Then lower your hands ...

... What happened? Did they merge — do they still merge — into one picture window? If so, is it closed, or ajar, or wide open? How big is it, how many centimeters does it measure? Does it have any frame, any limits at all? On present evidence, are you not this Single Eye (come on, you can count), this speckless and infinite wide-openness to the world? Is it anything like that pair of jellied peepholes out of which you are peeking at the world, according to that world?

TEST 2. PICTURE FRAMING
PART ONE

Our instrument for this experiment is called a mesoscope. Unlike a telescope which is a one-way instrument for observing far objects such as stars, and a microscope which is a one-way instrument for observing near objects such as cells, it's a two-way instrument for simultaneously observing middle-distance objects such as people, *together with their observer*. You will also need a mirror and, if possible, a friend at hand.

Frame your face with your hands, like this:

Your palms should be vertical. Your fingers should be horizontal and held up against your forehead.

Isn't what you are *looking at* — namely my drawing — entirely different from what you are *looking out of*? Isn't it true that, for you and on present evidence, your hands aren't framing a face at all? That they are framing space, just empty space that's keenly aware of itself as capacity for the scene ahead?

Now set up your mesoscope, this way. With your hands in the same position, go right up to the mirror on the wall and observe the one in there whose hands do frame a face — the face you are in the habit of calling yours.

Is there any similarity at all between the two "faces" on display in your mesoscope — the one at the far end so opaque and the one at the near end so transparent? Between the one you are looking at and the one you are looking out of? Isn't the near one what you are at center, your Reality, whereas the far one is what you look like out there — in fact just one of your countless regional appearances?

Take a little time to figure out further differences between these two framed pictures ...

... Well, how many of the following did you spot?

1. One is opaque, colored, textured and complex. The other is transparent, colorless, plain, simple, and uniform.
2. One, having the world for background, cannot face the world. The other must do so.
3. One distinguishes and sets you apart from all the rest. The other, having no personal distinguishing marks, embraces all, unites you to all.
4. One is visibly built to resist invasion and display only itself. The other is visibly wide open to whatever happens to be on show.
5. One is X years old. The other is 0.
6. One with no eyes is the seer. The other with eyes is the seen.
7. One blinks, thereby destroying and recreating the scene at will. The other, unable to blink, has no such power.

Now get your friend to read out loud to you, very slowly, these seven double-barreled propositions, while you are up against the mirror again, empty frame to filled frame. Make sure how many of the seven apply to you personally, to you, who alone, are in a position to prove them true or false. Why not trust what's clearly and wordlessly on show now, instead of the wordy and confused messages you have been getting to the contrary from outsiders all your life — outsiders who lack the necessary inside information? Why not take the data seriously at their face value — the value of that face over there at the far end of your mesoscope and the hugely different value of this "face" right here, where you are at the near end?

PART TWO

In this experiment your friend replaces the one in your mirror. Framing his face with his hands just as you are doing, he confronts you: so that, viewed from outside the mesoscope, you look like this:

Viewed from inside, however, what do you look like, when you drop all preconceptions? On present evidence, how many faces are in there? If one, where is it? Don't pretend you can't locate things, that you can't count! Are you face to face in there, or face to space? Dare to be your own authority: only you are in a position to settle the matter. Can you imagine what it would actually be like to confront someone face-to-face, symmetrically, with a mass of stuff for keeping him out? If you can, is it pitch black in there, congested, sticky? Be sensible! Have you ever, for a split second, solidified what you are looking out of? I'm not asking you what you feel or understand, but what you see.

Alas, we don't see what we see, but what Big Brother tells us to see. Fortunately, however, he is somewhat slow in the uptake. He hasn't yet extended his dominion to include our mesoscope, so we are free to go in and see what's so. Quick, then, before he catches up with this very special de-conditioning device!

But of course one glance at the clarity that's framed at the near end — at what Home is like — won't be enough to exorcise forever the Thing that has invaded and haunted your Home all your adult life. Though it vanishes on close inspection, it returns the instant your attention wanders. It is your wraith, your doppelganger, and if you don't

keep casting it out it will cast you out and be the death of you. Everything perishes.

PART THREE

To confirm your deathless and unhaunted No-thingness at center,
invite your friend to COME AND SEE. Ideally he should be a superhuman spaceman, bristling with optical and electronic instruments for
viewing you at all distances from light-years to nanometers. But in any
case he should be able to get near enough to lose practically all trace of
you. The final step he must leave to you who alone can make it all the
way home to the place you never really left, where the viewer is the
viewed and you coincide with you, where there remains nothing to
perish, where you are eccentric no longer. And where the one Nothing that you are neatly rounds off the many things (ranging from a
galaxy and a solar system and a planet and a human to cells and molecules and atoms and even more vacuous almost-nothings) that you
appear to be.

And so, between you, you set up a hospitable and broad-minded
science that no longer leaves the scientist as First Person outside in the
cold, but from the start accommodates the Subject as comfortably as
the object.

TEST 3. LOCATING MOTION

The world doesn't *tell* you that it obligingly stays still while you
rush around in it. That on the road it's *you* who are traveling north in
the fast lane of the highway, and *not* those mountains and foothills and
trees and cottages and telegraph poles that are traveling south, in the
slow and medium and fast lanes of the world. It doesn't need to
tell you. Who doubts it? It's obvious! Or is it?

Well, let's see. Your apparatus this time is a
motion detector. You make it up like this:

Hold it 20 centimeters away at shoulder
height, with one finger pointing in at what
sees and the other out at what's seen. Now
rotate clockwise on the spot, asking yourself *which finger is pointing at what in fact
is rotating*. Is it you or the room — ceiling, door, windows, pictures on the wall
— that's whizzing round counter-clock-

wise, on present evidence?

Was the evidence ever different? Can you do anything to exchange roles, and get the seer moving instead of the seen? If not, isn't this scientific discovery of yours wildly different from what the world tells you about yourself and the things you get up to? Wake up, do yourself justice! Establish your life on a uniquely stable footing.

Here, as put out by Hindu, Buddhist, Greek, Jewish, Christian and Muslim masters, and a noted physicist, are various aspects of the hypothesis we have been testing: which (let me remind you) is that you and I are the very opposite of what Common Sense, Big Brother's Brainwasher-in-Chief insists we are:

> KATHA UPANISHAD: God made the senses turn outwards, therefore a man looks outwards, not into himself. But now and again a daring soul, desiring immortality, has looked back and found himself.
>
> HUI-HAI: Do eyes and ears perceive? No. Your own Buddha Nature, being essentially pure and utterly still, is capable of this perception.
>
> ARISTOTLE: God is the unmoved mover of the world.
>
> ZOHAR: Blessed is the person who utterly surrenders his soul for the name of God to dwell therein and to establish therein its throne of glory.
>
> ST. BASIL THE GREAT: Man is a creature who has received the command to be God.
>
> IBN ARABI: Only God has seeing, hearing.
>
> ERWIN SCHRÖDINGER: Consciousness is a singular of which the plural is unknown.

Let's take those tricky terms Self and Buddha Nature and Consciousness and God to mean One that perceives Itself to be the individuality-transcending, changeless, ageless, boundless and motionless No-thing that is the seer and mover and container of all the things on show; the Reliable One, the Entirely Predictable. (By contrast, the hobgoblin of uncertainty bugs everything at the far end: there are a dozen reasons why Haley's Comet might not turn up.) Given this definition, I ask you: is our hypothesis proved? Can you reasonably dismiss the perdurable tradition that you — yes You, as revealed to Yourself at the near end of every instrument and situation — are none other than that August One, call It or Her or Him by whatever name you fancy?

And so this bold incursion of science into the field of religion not only leaves them the best of friends, but unites them in a holy matrimony which you can see for yourself is already fruitful. But if you still suspect you're only human after all, why not try a few of our other tests? They total about twenty, so far, and call upon other senses than vision. You will find full instructions about how to do most of them in my books.

As scientific experiments, of course, our tests remain cool and disinterested and not a bit holy. They are solely concerned with foundations, with our basis of hard and stubborn facts that are always easy to verify. Not with their personal or social consequences or religious or philosophical implications, all of which belong to the warm and cloud-wrapped superstructure of our world, where "facts" are malleable and nothing's clear-cut or exact, and you are as entitled to your opinion as I am to my maybe contrary opinion. But this is where we live, and naturally look to the meaning and consequences of our basic discoveries. To the emergent feeling, the thrill, the healing, the ever-changing payoff. For example, having discovered, courtesy of our mesoscope, that I'm built *open* for you, I may well go on to declare — to sing and to shout! — that I'm built *for loving* you, that the space which I am is nothing without you — you, just as you are — to fill it, and that our confrontation is the lie which shall run and ruin our lives no longer. Again, on the road, waking at last to the glaringly obvious fact that it's the countryside and never me that's behaving frantically, I'm apt to find myself enjoying a new and pleasurable tranquillity. Also new powers: *Who* is it that, instead of driving his Land Rover, finds himself driving his Land? Or again, ceasing to overlook the Clear Eye with which I have always seen the world, I'm all set to rediscover the morning brilliance of the world, the glowing colors and sounds and scents and tastes that I reveled in as a child. Yet again (and above all) the more steadily I gaze at the One that's nearest and clearest, the more it turns out to be the dearest, more me than myself, the Resource that never *really* lets me down. The Wide Awake One that — though homely and obvious and transparent through and through — fills me with worship and wonder at the mystery of its self-origination. Who shall set limits to the bright blessings that can arise from our growing willingness to trust what we see, instead of what we're told to see?

Yes of course, the fabulous superstructure of our world is all-important. Hence our distress at its falling apart — not from lack of sound foundations but from our failure to acknowledge and build on them.

Four hundred years ago Galileo Galilei, along with a handful of other European intellectuals, succumbed to an attack of childlikeness, of inspired idiocy. Taking leave of their wits, they came to their senses. To find out what was going on they dared to *look* instead of *looking it up* in the Bible or Aristotle or the Fathers of the Church, or *thinking it up* in their studies. Actually to look and see, for instance, whether heavy stones *do* fall faster than light ones. That one word LOOK! was enough to trigger the scientific revolution that has transformed our lives beyond recognition — for better and for worse. And now, four centuries on, we desperately need to invoke the same magic word, to pronounce the same spelling, but extending it to LOOK ROUND! The well-meaning but overrated habit of scrutinizing what's on show at the far end of our instrument, for every least hint about what might be here at the near end, is no substitute whatsoever for looking here, for the quite easy feat of looking round without turning round. The time has come for attending to what's *simultaneously* on show at *both* ends of our telemicro-mesoscopes, for panoramic instead of tunnel vision. Thanks to Galileo and successors, superstition is on the run from the far end, but all the more dug in at the near end, which it blocks with a fictitious observing thing — as if any *thing* could observe anything, or take in and respond to any appearance without disappearing in its favor, or get the picture without being the screen!

And so this deep and vast and superstition-ridden region is opened up to a science which has hitherto, and with good reason, insisted that subjectivity is the enemy of objectivity. What an opportunity for science to give rein at last to its own splendidly uninhibited spirit which is an even-handed and unbiased humility in the face of *all* the evidence, coming from *whatever* direction, given at *no* distance from the observer! After all, it isn't as if the promise of precision and predictability and practicality, plus the "wow!" of never-ending discovery, were to be found only at the *far* end of our instrument, in the object and never the Subject. And the reason why we can confidently be objective about the Subject is that, at our deepest level, we find them merging in the First Person Singular who, as scientist par excellence, takes himself to be his own most penetrable and revealing specimen.

Surely it's only to be expected that a one-directional gaze, taking in no more than half the scene at most, should find in it all sorts of obscurities and loose ends and contradictions which the other half could light up and tie up and even clear up. An outstanding example is the conundrum of the cosmic status of the scientist himself, which we have addressed. In *The Science of the First Person* I give some others: in fact thirty-seven instances of how 360-degree vision can make sense of the nonsenses that plague 180-degree vision, not to mention narrower angles.

And not only make sense but make history. Systematic two-way attention could trigger an even more radical revolution than the one triggered by Galileo and his contemporaries, and certainly a more environment-friendly and species-friendly and person-friendly revolution. Will it come off? There are grounds for hope. Already those who are instigating the two-way scientific revolution are at least as numerous and dedicated as those who instigated the one-way scientific revolution of the sixteenth-century onwards. To the old motives of inquisitiveness and practical utility, moreover, is added the new motive of stern necessity, of Humanity's struggle to survive its suicidal tendencies. Every day it becomes more apparent that "we must love one another or die."

This is the challenge we face. Shall we or shan't we give love a chance, by ceasing to deny that at base we are built for it? Our true foundations are marvelously sound. Shall you, shall I, build securely on them, or continue to jerry-build on a quicksand of lies? In particular, on the lie that *I'm not what I am, which I see is wide open to you, but what I look like, which isn't?*

That monstrous but rarely challenged lie is what Big Brother warns me I'd better believe — or else … Yes, he, too, has his apparatus, his instruments of persuasion. He confronted Galileo with the rack and the thumbscrew, forcing him to recant. Nowadays his techniques — which rely on our well-based fear that to look within is to disappear, and our baseless fear that this means annihilation — are more subtle and efficient. Nevertheless the dauntless spirit of science burns bright and clear in everyone who sees that to disappear as a particular thing is to reappear instantly as the No-thing that is the imperishable Home of all that perishes, and that to die now is to die never.

At the near end, and ultimately, the science of liberation and the liberation of science are inseparable.

LET'S HAVE AN
OUT-OF-THE-BODY
EXPERIENCE

I promise you an out-of-the-body experience before you come to the end of this chapter.

But before we get *out* of our bodies we need to take a look at what it means to be *in* them. Or simply to *be* them. Let's start with the last of these three alternatives, and work back.

1. BEING THE BODY

To find out what's going on we have only to listen to the way we talk. "He touched me." "I am fairly tall." "I weigh a hundred and fifty pounds." "I came here from London." "I was born in 1940, which makes me middle-aged." "When I die I want to be cremated." And so on.

In all such statements (and what a large part of our talk they constitute!), I am without any doubt or qualification identifying myself with my body. What happens to it happens to me. What it does I do. Its achievements and shortcomings, its beginning and ending, are mine. And the law itself, following the lead of common sense, agrees. It accuses me of doing what my hand does — stealing, wounding, killing, whatever — and punishes me accordingly. It would be of little use pleading that I'm not my body, and what this hand gets up to is none of my business. At best, I'd find myself in a hospital for the criminally insane instead of in prison.

2. BEING IN THE BODY

Maybe I go on to explain that this common-sense identification with the body is no more than a useful — perhaps indispensable — social fiction, and the truth is that I am *not* my body and have never been my body. Instead, I am *in* my body. All the same, what this means isn't very clear to me. Presumably what I mean is that I'm some kind of ghost or goblin or spook who is temporally trapped or entombed somewhere inside this 150 pounds of flesh and blood. Or am I everywhere in the thing, except in a few insignificant parts like nails and hair? In that case I'm a prison-shaped prisoner, and a shocking case of over-crowding. Anyway, it seems I'm a most mysterious spook that animates this most mysterious corpse in a most mysterious fashion, and tells itself the following story:

"Since birth I have been incarnated, confined in this 'house of clay.' But soon it will break up and 'give up the ghost,' and I shall go free. Then one of five things is going to happen to me. I may break up at the same time. I may hang around for a while, haunting the house I lived in or the graveyard my body was buried in, before finally coming to an end. I may ascend to my happy home in heaven. I may descend to a less comfortable place. Or, finally, I may look around for another 'house of clay' — a newborn baby, perhaps — to inhabit." Which of these five alternatives will come to pass is anyone's guess. An uncertain and not very satisfactory state of affairs, I think you will agree. So we turn now to our third alternative.

3. BEING OUT OF THE BODY

According to this third view I neither *am* my body nor *in* it. On the contrary, it — along with the rest of my world — is *in me*. No guesswork this time, no conforming to social fictions: I see clearly that I'm not this body-thing nor am I its inhabitant. I am no-thing whatever. These sensations of warmth and pressure and pain and pleasure, these tastes and smells and touches and sounds, these moving colored shapes which I call my hands and feet, that curious creature staring fixedly at me out of my mirror, and all the rest — what are they but a passing show going on in the all-embracing Space which I am? They are like flocks of birds flying through my Air and leaving no trails, like shoals of fish swimming in my Ocean without raising a ripple, like a succession of actors and actresses appearing on my television and disappearing again without ever leaving a mark on it.

"Bully for you," I can hear you saying, "but you promised *me* an out-of-the-body experience."

Here it is, preceded by a warning. I didn't promise a peak experience, or a mystical experience, or anything out of the ordinary.

Look at the hand that's now holding the book open at this page, and answer, on present evidence and as honestly as possible, the following questions:

Am I in that thumb but outside the page it's pressing on?

If so, what's it like in there? Dark, wet, sticky?

Have I any inside information whatsoever about the structure or constituents of that thumb or that page, or is it a fact that I'm in no position to say?

If I'm outside that thumb and hand and arm and the rest of my body, how big am I?

Am I not at large and without any boundaries?

I think I can hear you saying: "All right. So far I'm with you. All the same, I'm more inside my body than yours."

"Don't be so sure of that," I reply, "until you have conducted the following experiment."

Make a tangle of your ten fingers with those of a friend, like this:

Carefully examine the result, and answer, on present evidence, these questions:

Am I more in some of those fingers than others?

Or are they all equally in me?

Including those that hurt when pricked and those that don't?

Being in the spiritual line of business, I'm occasionally asked about my out-of-the-body experiences. I can only reply that I'm having one right now, and that I never had any other sort. What's more, I find it hard to imagine what an *in*-the-body-experience would be like. I'm still looking for someone to tell me. What about you?

Let's not cheat ourselves. This chapter doesn't describe three ways in which we may relate to the body — *being* that hugely complex bag of tricks, or *being* in it, or containing *it*. There's only one way. We have no option. Only the last of these three applies to oneself, or makes any sense at all. The other "ways" are hearsay, unexamined dogmas, in fact plain lies about oneself that one has been too lazy or too timid to challenge. It's never practical or healthy to live from a lie of any sort, but when that lie is about one's essential Nature — look out! Or rather, look in! Attend, as if for the first time, to the one Spot in the world that only you are in a position to inspect, to the Point that only you have inside information about, and witness its immediate explosion to worldwide dimensions. Look for yourself. Don't take my word for it. At this moment, are you incarcerated in an airless prison, solid all the way through, wall to wall? Or are you at large and free ranging, so wide open and lightsome that all the winds of God blow through you? How amazing it is that you should ever have imagined otherwise!

Nevertheless you may well, at this point, raise what seems like a very serious objection: "To discount, if not to write off altogether the body in favor of the mind and spirit (as so many have done, and you appear to be doing in this chapter) must be bad for the body — if not for the other two as well. Sensitive to adverse criticism, the body hates being snubbed, and is likely to retaliate with disease and premature aging."

In reply, let me strike a personal — a first-personal note. Over the past half-century I have found that cultivating the habit of seeing that one is clear of one's body, honors and refreshes and invigorates it, and my observation of others backs up this view. So that — paradoxical, if you like — one becomes *more* physical, more alive and alert, and the process of aging is slowed down. Why is that? The answer is quite simple. Because it's Nature's way, because it goes by the evidence. And relying on the given facts rather than preconceptions is always a sound policy.

The reason why you were so much more agile and surefooted at five than you will be (or are) at fifty-five is that you hadn't yet learned to inhabit your body and monitor its movements. Instead of interfering with its marvelous know-how, you let it get on with its job. Why does your cat move so gracefully, never putting a paw wrong? Because, for herself, she's not a cat at all, not packaged in a cat-shaped container. Because she's at large, not self-occupied but occupied with mice and birds and other cats, and the milk that regularly appears in her saucer. In short, because her life is one great out-of-the-body experience.

For us, too, an occasional out-of-the-body experience isn't nearly enough. To be fully operative it needs to approach the cat's, which is constant and unself-conscious. Meantime it's for deliberately practicing. Curiously enough, it's practiced by repeatedly venturing *inside* your body, and discovering there your boundless clarity and the striking absence of all that anatomy. For us humans, incarnation is excarnation, and the way out of the body is the way in. What was wrong with alternatives (1) *Being the body* and (2) *Being in the body* was the notion that, in and for oneself, one is a limited thing stuffed with a lot of even more limited things. Correct the false notion that you are an example of the taxidermist's art, and you will find that all three alternatives come to the same thing. Which isn't a thing at all, but immense and brilliantly conscious capacity for everything under and above the sun.

One last query you may feel like raising: "If the belief that I am, or am lodged in, this 'too too solid flesh,' is such a damaging lie, how is it that we — the millions that are so sure of its truth — get by as well as we do? Can you be sure it does us all that harm? There must be something to be said for a fiction so universal and so useful that it goes virtually unchallenged. *Vox populi, vox Dei.*"

To which I reply: *Vox populi* — alias common sense — is the megaphone that blares out all the delusions that plague our species, and the one we have been examining is basic. As for *vox Dei*, listen to the God-seers who are His spokespeople, such as Ramana Maharshi:

- Are you in the world, or is the world in you?
- Man considers himself limited and there arises the trouble. The idea is wrong. He can see it for himself.
- "I am the body" is the cause of all the mischief. This delusion must go. That is Realization.
- Grief exists only so long as one considers oneself to be of definite form.
- Identification of the Self with the body is the real

THE NATURE
OF THE
PHYSICAL WORLD

Science — or rather, science misunderstood and gone haywire — has come up with a great deal of unscientific nonsense in its time. And the most prevalent, the most silly, the most absurd piece of pseudo-scientific nonsense is the dogma that consciousness is a by-product of matter — a kind of incidental and accidental effluvium or subtle radiation that matter gives off when it gets sufficiently complex, as in human brains. The one thing led to the other, as if brains happened to grow a bump of consciousness in addition to the other bumps! As if the protuberance on the top of the head of images of the Buddha were the bump of that superconsciousness which he called enlightenment! In the beginning was a lot of stuff, and in the course of time it got around to noticing itself! Clever stuff! Wonder of wonders, object gives birth to subject. Are we astounded at such a maculate Conception and Nativity? Not at all. We take it in our stride. The primacy of matter over spirit is simply taken for granted. It is among the least challenged of the myths we live by.

That things should produce awareness of things — and by chance, at that — is, when you think of it, quite weird. It's like supposing that the movie-projector is operated by one of the actors on the screen. Equally odd is the notion that the subject can be examined from outside as if it were some kind of object. How can the subject be discovered except from within, by subjectivity itself? In any case there's not a particle of evidence of material things giving rise to consciousness. No one has ever observed it happen, or explained what to look for. In fact, the very idea is nonsensical.

What *is* a material object, according to science itself? It is a collection of phenomena (from the Greek *phainein*, to show), a set of regional appearances/pictures/readings which the scientist picks up and pieces together as he hovers round the "thing" he's surveying from various angles, at various distances, with the help of various instruments. What these regional appearances are appearances of, what nestles at their center, is hidden from him. However close he gets to that thing so-called, he remains too far off to say what it really is, intrinsically, at no distance from itself. The scientist, as such, is an outsider.

But he does have two clues to what's inside:

1. His first clue is that the nearer he gets to the thing the less "thingy" and the more empty it becomes. Progressively stripping it of assets, he comes to regions where all that remains of that seemingly solid object is space haunted by twists of energy, so to speak. Beauty and ugliness, utility, life, color, opacity, shape, even precise location — all are left behind by the approaching observer. There's not a quality or function that will stand up to close inspection. It is distance that lends these enchantments. Go up to anything and you lose it.

    But just a minute! Who goes up to that thing and loses it? Who registers the dismantling and disappearance of the object and its reduction to virtual emptiness? Why, the scientist himself, of course, as consciousness. He leaves all behind except awareness. You could say he takes it with him wherever he goes, because that is what he is. It's impossible for him to explore the physical world of cells and molecules and atoms and particles and leave it merely physical: his active presence there infects it through and through and at every level with spirit. As for the space that underlies all, how could his awareness of it be separated from that space? Just as there's no way of entering an *empty* house, so there's no way of contemplating mindless space. No wonder subatomic physics is forced by the facts to bring the observer into the picture. In fact, while the picture fades on ever closer inspection, the consciousness that illuminates it shines all the more brightly. Matter dissolves in favor of spirit.

    Let me put it in another — and I think better — way. Things can be moved and carried around. Not so consciousness of things. It isn't a torch which the scientist takes along with him to shine on things, or an air freshener he sprays them with, or a laser beam he directs at them. Wherever he goes it's already there, inseparable from the very nature of those things. If for the word *consciousness* or *spirit* I read *God* (and there are many worse names for It) then I can say with the Psalmist:

> Whither shall I go from thy spirit, or whither shall I
> flee from thy presence?
> If I ascend up into heaven, thou art there: if I make
> my bed in hell, behold thou art there.
> If I take the wings of the morning, and dwell in the
> uttermost parts of the sea,
> Even there shall thy hand lead me, and thy right
> hand shall hold me.

In short, spirit or consciousness underlies all, and there is no such thing as the merely physical. A phenomenon or regional appearance by itself, without a central reality of which it is an appearance — what sort of nonsense is that, for heaven's sake?

2.   There exist two distinct kinds of things (so-called) which are available for the scientist's inspection — the observed thing and the observing thing. That is to say, other bodies, and his own body. We have just seen to what conclusions his examination of other bodies leads. Now let us find out whether they are confirmed by his examination of his own body, the specimen he carries around with him all the while.

Here, nearer than near, is his second clue to what things really are, as distinct from what they look like at a distance. Here is his very own sample lump of matter, always handy, requiring no laboratory or instruments for its most searching examination, constantly reporting on its true and intrinsic nature, transparent through and through to his direct inspection. If (and it's a very big if) he takes seriously this unique and precious sample — if and when he dares to look at what he's looking out of, inspecting from inside that one thing on which he is the final authority — why then he finds it to be quite empty, and in fact no kind of thing at all. A nothing keenly aware of itself as just that. Such is the view of himself at no distance from himself, provided he is honest and attentive enough. Which is to say, truly scientific.

Notice how nicely these two clues confirm each other. Whether looked at from outside or inside, bodies dissolve, matter vanishes, spirit remains — once we bother to go into the matter. "Spirit is the living body seen from within, and the body is the outer manifestation of the living spirit." Extend this statement by Carl Jung to all bodies from electrons to galaxies, and you have the ultimate physics.

To understand the primacy of spirit is good. To realize it, to see it, wordlessly to experience it, to be it without thinking about it — this is incomparably better. And incomparably easier: in fact, understanding must always be *about* its object, hovering round and about it and never gaining admittance. That is why the rest of this chapter is a heartfelt invitation to the reader to do one or two little experiments, which will surely lead to this direct perception of what would otherwise remain a mere set of lifeless concepts.

Observe this thing you are now holding. What in reality is this object called "book"? I mean this actual wad of paper with printing. There it is, a solid enough lump of stuff a few inches wide and long and less than an inch thick, weighing rather less than a pound, covered with (I trust) meaningful black marks on a white surface. Now where are these meaningful patterns that you are currently taking in? Are they over there, some 12 inches away, or are they where you are?

Well, let's put the matter to the test. Go right up to the page and see. Apply your eye to this printing, as if you were putting on a contact lens. Yes please, all the way. If you feel a bit ridiculous, remember what's at stake. Namely Reality itself, and your status within it. Go on …

What did you see? I venture to say that what you found there was not meaningful sentences, not loose words, not a string of letters, not even fuzzy black marks on a white ground, but an illegible blur. And, on contact, nothing at all. You lost everything, but you didn't lose consciousness. It was the book, not you, that passed away. The nothing you found wasn't just nothing at all — whatever that monster could be — it was Nothing but Awareness. "There is a Light by which things are seen," says Ramana Maharshi, "if divested of things the Light alone remains."

So much for where these printed words are coming from. Where are they going to? Who is reading them now, on present evidence? What is taking them in? In your own firsthand experience at this moment, is it a solid, rounded, hairy thing with two peepholes in it? Only you — you who are your own closest inspector — are in a position to say. Again, isn't it true that what you go right up to you lose? You certainly go all the way to you. So it's no wonder that you vanish, just as the page did, leaving only awareness. Intrinsically, then, the Reader is the same as the Read, and none other than Spirit which is indivisible. To put it picturesquely, this page of printing is a letter from Spirit to Spirit, a love-letter from You to You. And, of course, what's true of this page is true of the other pages in this book when you come to them, and of the hands that are now holding it, and of the furniture in the room, and of all that's going on outside. They are views of You, messages from You, displayed to You. At root, all you perceive is Yourself, heavily disguised as someone else, for your entertainment and refreshment.

It would be difficult to overstate the practical importance of this discovery, its consequences for everyday living. All alienation, all separation, the many-sided threat of hostile things and persons and situations — these are no more than bad dreams. All is You. How could you fear Yourself? How could you despise, resent, be bored by Yourself? How could you not love Yourself?

All this and more than this. Everything you see and hear and handle is something you want to say to yourself, something well worth saying, something significant — even if it's only about an oncoming bus. There can be no dreadful or garbled or meaningless messages from you to You. News about You, read by You is good news, however bad it may sound to the hearer who is deaf to its Source and Destiny in himself as Spirit. To him Ramana says: "The imperfection appears to you. God is perfection. His work also is perfection. But you see it as imperfection because of your wrong identification ... Find out if you are physical."

In conclusion, then, the spirit which is one and the same in all beings is the true nature of what we take to be the physical world. Things as such have no substance and no reality and no power at all. You could call them pictures of God held up by God for his own inspection, and in themselves less than paper-thin. All you have to do to live from this realization is to go on seeing who's doing it. And I mean *seeing*, not understanding.

HOW
TO BE
HAPPY

Samsara (the world of objects) is sorrow.

Men want absolute and permanent happiness. This does not reside in objects but in the Absolute. It is Peace, free from pain and pleasure. It is a neutral state.

Self-realization is Bliss.

Bliss is not something to be acquired. You are always Bliss... get rid of your ignorance which makes you think you are other than Bliss.

Happiness is inherent and not due to external causes. One must realize Oneself in order to open the store of unalloyed happiness.
— FROM *Talks with Sri Ramana Maharshi*

One of the inalienable rights of man, we are assured, is the pursuit of happiness. Yes indeed! But it is a right that is exercised more in talk than in action — effective action. Are we, in fact, serious about this pursuit? Of course we all say we want to be happy. Do we mean what we say? The truth is that our behavior, the way we go all out for happiness, makes quite sure it will get away. So unpractical we are in this search — so unwilling to profit by the advice of Sages like Ramana and by our own and others' oft-repeated failures — that it looks as if we were pursuing misery instead of happiness. Sure enough, we catch up with *that* quarry!

And yet it remains true that we want to be happy and not wretched. Otherwise those two words — our very lives — make no sense at all.

In short, we are thoroughly confused about the problem. It is our purpose in this chapter, with the help of Maharshi and other sages, to remove this confusion; to be very clear about how to be happy — so clear that we have no excuse for being miserable anymore.

All the many recipes for happiness reduce to three. Let us call them (1) The Common-sensible Recipe, (2) The Uncommon-sensible Recipe, and (3) The Sensible Recipe, which seems nonsense till you put it to the test.

THE COMMON-SENSIBLE RECIPE FOR HAPPINESS IS GETTING WHAT YOU WANT

For instance, at the "lowest" or most popular level of happiness means getting possessions, money, skills, reputation, power, and so forth — and getting more and more of it all the time. In a phrase, ongoing personal success.

At "middle levels", happiness means striving successfully for the well-being of one's family, sect, political party, nation, race, species — culminating, one hopes, in a much happier state of affairs, if not in some kind of New Jerusalem or Utopia, here on earth.

At the "highest level," happiness means working for the salvation of the whole world, the liberation of all beings — and getting some results.

Though so "ignoble" at its lowest and most popular levels, and so "noble" at its highest and least popular levels, this recipe comes to the same thing throughout — namely success, *getting what you want*.

As a recipe it seems sensible enough, but recipes happen to be inedible. The proof of the recipe is the pudding, and the proof of the pudding is the eating. Do we, in practice, get enough pudding this way to satisfy our hunger? Enough possessions, security, affection, influence, power, whether for our personal selves or for those larger selves called family, or nation, or sect, or species? Notoriously this getting is addictive, so that the more we accumulate the more we demand, and the thing that would make us "really happy" recedes at least as fast as our advance towards it. Nothing fails like success. The suicide rate goes up rather than down in affluent societies, and in the more "successful" groups within those societies. But of course everyone knows that great possessions and power bring little satisfaction. And no wonder: their maintenance gets more and more difficult as they grow, the prospect of their loss more and more worrying, their actual loss more and more painful. What fleeting pleasure they give lies more in the getting than in the having.

The ordinary man aims less high. Whether from necessity, or fear, or lack of drive, or native shrewdness, he plays for lower stakes. At best, he avoids extremes of pain and pleasure; at worst, he becomes a vegetable. For it is the very nature of what we *have* — whether it be little or much — to be insufficient. And it is in the very nature of what we *do* — whether it be petty or heroic or enlightened — to leave us unfulfilled. Necessary though they are, neither having nor doing will cure our sadness.

Altruism doesn't help here. Clearly the anxieties and disappointments of the public-minded citizen — of the one who seeks the welfare of his city, his nation, mankind itself — aren't less severe than those of the averagely selfish citizen. Nor are they, strictly speaking, less "selfish." After all, the Nazis submerged their personal selves in a suprapersonal one.

But what of the "highest" level — working for the salvation or enlightenment of the world? Is this the way to be happy? Jesus wept, and we know how the Man of Sorrows died. Anyone who takes on such a job is asking for trouble, as history shows. The fundamental reason is that his happiness doesn't really consist in getting what he wants, even if he gets it.

In short, however we look at it, our first recipe for happiness looks good but turns out to be otherwise. So let's try our second.

THE UNCOMMON-SENSIBLE RECIPE FOR HAPPINESS IS WANTING WHAT YOU GET

One of the finest advocates of this recipe (which, please note, is the precise opposite of our first recipe) is Jean-Pierre de Caussade, who writes: "If people knew the merit in what each moment of the day brings them ... and that the true philosopher's stone is submission to the designs of God, transmuting into fine gold all their occupations, their worries and their sufferings, how happy they would be."

In one way or another, all the great spiritual traditions are agreed about the need for "self-abandonment to the divine Providence." The very word *Islam* means submission to the will of Allah. Which is not, for the proficient Sufi, resignation or mere obedience, but full identification with the divine will, so that he actively chooses what that will ordains. How could he be unhappy, in that case? Again, according to the Buddha, it is desire or craving which causes suffering, and the extinction of desire is the end of suffering. And Ramana Maharshi: "Desirelessness is God."

When you are personally desireless, when you choose what is instead of what *isn't*, when you want what you get no matter what it's like, when God's will expressed in your circumstances becomes precisely your will, why then you are Him! It's as simple as that.

Simple for me to write and for you to read and understand. But hard to put into practice, to live. Come on, let's be practical! *How* to give up our personal desires to the point of actually wanting those nasty things we are so apt to get? By desiring desirelessness so earnestly that we start training to achieve it? By craving and going all out for some kind of sainthood? Could anything be crazier? What's the sense in accepting everything except your humanness, with all its cravings? In any case, how on earth can you force yourself to stop wanting what you want? Suppose your house catches fire, your child is burned to death, you go bankrupt, your health cracks up (these things are happening to people all the while), and tell me (and them) how you would go about welcoming those events.

And so, for the second time, we have a seemingly insoluble problem on our hands: in fact, the problem of our lives. We who are not saints have still to find a recipe for happiness that we can actually use right now, just as we are. Well, let's see whether our third and final recipe works.

THE SENSIBLE RECIPE FOR HAPPINESS IS SEEING WHAT YOU'VE GOT

What if you were happy already — were happiness itself — and never noticed the fact? What if this frantic search for happiness elsewhere blinds you to the searcher's True Nature which is bliss itself?

Sri Nisargadatta is sure of the answer, and certainly doesn't mince matters. "Nothing can make you happier than you are. All search for happiness is misery and leads to more misery. The only happiness worth the name is the natural happiness of conscious being." This, and the quotations from Ramana Maharshi that preface this chapter, together with the teaching of the long line of seers and sages who have indissolubly linked *ananda* (Bliss) with *sat* (Being) and *chit* (Awareness), and certainly the experience of this writer, all insist that the true recipe for happiness is seeing Who you really are, and enjoying your very Nature as unalloyed Bliss.

How, then, to see Who you really are? In fact, it's easier to see than anything else! Just look at What you are looking out of at this moment, at what's your side of these printed words, and see Nothing — no shape or form, no complexity, no color, no texture, no opacity, no limits, no movement — nothing but Awareness.

But does this seeing into your Self-nature (and it's something you can't do wrong) mean that you want things to happen as they do happen? Well, who is responsible for them? Who you really, really are creates the world, and presumably isn't regretting any of it.

Those who have actually tried it find that this last recipe for happiness is the one that works. What's more, it makes the other two work. Consistently seeing Who you really are, you want what you get and get what you want. Again, this isn't for believing but for testing.

In his *Ethics* the great Greek philosopher Aristotle concluded that happiness is some form of *theoria*, which means a looking-at, a viewing, a beholding. That's to say, not a subjective state for achieving one day but an objective reality for enjoying right now. A reality we can't get rid of no matter how we try.

THE
THREE
WISHES

Once upon a time there was a poor woodsman who lived with his wife in the forest. One day, when he was cutting logs by a stream, he was startled to hear someone crying, and even more startled to find it was a fairy sitting on the bank of the stream bemoaning the fact that he couldn't get across. Lifting him onto his shoulder, the woodsman waded the stream and set the little fellow down gently on the other bank. "As a reward for your kindness," said the fairy, "I grant you three wishes." That evening, over their humble meal, the woodsman told his wife about the fairy and the three wishes, and they discussed at length what boons to ask for. "While we're making up our minds," said the woodsman, "I certainly could do with a sausage to go with this dry bread." And immediately a fine sausage landed on the table. His wife, furious at him for wasting a wish on something so trivial instead of a sack of gold, couldn't help blurting out, "You stupid old man! You deserve to have this miserable sausage growing at the end of your miserable nose!" And at once there it was, dangling from the poor man's nose. Well, after further argument and mutual recrimination, they agreed that their third and last wish must be to get rid of the sausage and restore the situation to normal. And so it happened. The three wishes were indeed granted as the good fairy had promised, yet in the end they left everything unchanged. The man and his wife got what they finally decided on, which left the normal routine of their simple lives unchanged. But with this difference: *it was their choice.*

What a wasted opportunity! Or was it? Was all lost by that foolish couple? Or could there have been more to that third wish than just repairing a desperate situation? Was it, after all, and in spite of their silliness, the wisest and most rewarding wish they could have made, the true sack of gold? The one we all need to make, as well as the one we are all granted?

Various lessons can be learned from this well-known folktale. The one offered here is as follows. We are indeed granted three wishes. The first and overt one is that we get something we consciously want. The second and hidden wish is that, along with that something, we get the shadow side of it without which it's a mere phantom — it's negative side or antithesis — which we don't consciously want. Far from it! The third and even more hidden wish is that we get all of the things — both "good" and "bad" — everything that happens to us, much of which our surface mind vaguely resents and some of which it hates and fears. Evidently this third and last wish is the only one that is always granted in full.

And not at all, evidently, is it — whether or not we ever get round to admitting it — the one that is our deepest desire. The truth is that we have already chosen that our world shall be exactly as it is at this moment, but are unaware of having made this momentous choice. We repress it, and the symptoms of repression afflict us. We disclaim responsibility and wash our hands of the whole tragi-comic affair — and pay the heavy price. And so it comes about that our true life's work and our healing is to end that repression, raising to consciousness our heartfelt acceptance of the world just as it impinges on us. That, in brief, is our interpretation of the story of the woodsman's three wishes.

The masters of the spiritual life are in agreement. "God is telling you," says Jean-Pierre de Caussade, "that if you abandon all restraint, *carry your wishes to their furthest limits*, open your heart boundlessly, there is not a single moment when you will not find all you could possibly desire. The present moment holds infinite riches beyond your wildest dreams."

On the face of it, this is extravagant talk, wish-fulfilling nonsense that's far too good to be true. Such wild optimism, apparently so contrary to common sense and to our experience of life itself, certainly isn't to be taken blindly on trust. It demands rigorous testing and proof, if it's to be credited at all. And most of us, floundering — if not yet drowning — in a raging sea of disappointments and frustrations, are going to take a lot of convincing.

In the rest of this chapter, I want to put to you some reasons for concluding that, amazingly, de Caussade was altogether right to claim that, when we let ourselves go (repeat, when we let ourselves go) and push our wishes beyond our surface consciousness to their as-yet-unconscious limit, we shall find them at once perfectly fulfilled. That, in fact, the reason we don't get what we want is that we don't want enough; that our demands, like those of the woodsman and his wife, are infinitely too modest.

Only get your Identity right, and the rest comes right. Whatever your problem, the only real answer to it is to see whose problem it is. The answer to the problem of your will — of what you want and how to get it — is no exception. Who is the one that demands this and refuses that? Who is this one really and truly? Solve that riddle and you have solved the riddle of what you *really* wish for, and how to be *really* sure of getting it.

Put it like this: you have two identities, one apparent and provisional and the other real and for good. In appearance, as you are seen by other people (looking at you from a distance) you certainly are a something — something shaped, confined within distinct boundaries, perfectly opaque, multicolored, local and not all over the place, hugely complex, moving around, going for this and avoiding that, and moreover just one of countless similarly limited and very choosy creatures. But *in reality*, as you see yourself (looking at yourself from no distance) you are ...? Well, why not just look and see, right now? Isn't it a fact — an amazing and crucial fact — that in your own present experience you are the very opposite of how you strike others, and of how you struck yourself before you got around to looking for yourself? That instead of being a thing among things you are Space for things — including, just now, these printed words, this page, the hands holding the book, and their fuzzy background? Only you are in a position to answer the all-important question of what's your side of the scene, of whatever's occurring to you. If, in all honesty, you perceive yourself to be a something here confronting a lot of somethings there, why of course you should stick to your view: you are the sole authority on your experience of you. Only, in that case, I suggest you take a short break from reading, and devote it to re-examining the spot you occupy, just in case you discover that, after all, it's occupied by others and not by you at all!

But if you do indeed find that you are No-thing where you are, if

you agree that you are Space, Accommodation for whatever you happen to be occupied with, why then the problem of your will — of getting your own way — is solved. In reality you have no will, seeing that
Space has no needs and makes no demands. As Space you are self-
sufficient, whereas none of the bodies, of the visible bits and pieces of
your own body, none of the limited objects coming and going in your
Space is self-sufficient. Their needs are insatiable; they must continually pursue what makes for their survival and resist what makes for
their destruction. All this purposive behavior of course characterizes
you also as the limited object you appear to be when looked at from
outside, but never you as the unlimited Subject you really are when
looked at from inside. As Capacity for objects you the Subject are freed
from them all, forever the same, unstainable, invulnerable. Obviously
this self-aware Emptiness which you now clearly perceive yourself to be
doesn't prefer some of its contents to others. It has no favorites, no
preferences, no opinions, no plots or plans, no comments at all to
make. Like a mirror it accepts dirty things as readily as clean ones, ugly
things as uncritically as beautiful ones, tragic things as coolly as joyful
ones, and none of them leaves any trace. As your true Self you have no
likes or dislikes, which in practice is only another way of saying that in
the last resort all happens to your liking. Inevitably so, seeing that
Who you are is responsible for what is. There's a paradox here, of
course: one which Angelus Silesius noted when he wrote, "We pray *Thy
will be done*. But He has no will. He is Stillness alone." As Him, you have
it both ways. You get what you want because you want what you get.
Truly there's no other will than yours — you Who are without will!

It may well seem to you that we have now left behind the firm
ground of direct and indubitable experience and taken off into the
nebulous realm of pious speculation. In what follows I hope to show
that, on the contrary, it all makes good sense.

Let's look more carefully into the question of how many wills there
really are. Consider the human body. It's made up of billions of creatures called cells, each of which is born and flourishes and dies inde-
pendently of the life of the body as a whole. Each competes with the
others for the available nourishment, each follows unswervingly its
characteristic behavior pattern, each strives for its own survival regardless of the others. And the end result of all this unbridled individual-
ism? Wonder of wonders, in spite of themselves these myriads of separate lives add up to a single life of a higher order — that of the whole

man. When he walks and talks and minds his own business, it's thanks to his horde of subordinates (cells comprising his vocal chords, tongue, lips, leg muscles, etcetera), each minding its own business, which is nothing like his. Nor does this magical process of will-transmutation begin and end here, of course. The integration of divergent parts into wholes of a higher order goes on at every level — particles into atoms, atoms into molecules, molecules into cells, cells into plants and animals and humans, and so on upwards till in the end the entire hierarchy of parts and wholes culminates in the Whole. In the Whole that alone is perfectly *whole* and self-contained and dependent on nothing external. The Universe itself constitutes a single Super-organism, the only true Individual, compounded of and reconciling and unifying the hugely divergent drives and intentions and activities of its components at every level, including the human. De Caussade puts it beautifully: "Divine action cleanses the universe, pervading and flowing over all creatures."

How does man dovetail into this grand cosmic design? Viewing him from within as Subject, we have already found him to be the Nothing that includes Every-thing — in a word, the Whole. And now, viewing him from outside as an object, as the thing provisionally called a human being, we find that that thing isn't itself without the backing of the rest of things belonging to all levels. What is man, indeed, without the world of cells, molecules, atoms, and particles that comprise him from within and below and without the world of other organisms, of Earth and Sun and Stars that sustain him from without and above? He's not himself without them. The *whole* man is the Whole. Nothing less is viable, all there. However you look at him, then, whether from inside or outside, in the last resort he is the all-inclusive Being that organizes the divergent wills of all beings into a single will. It's called God's will, and it is none other than your will when you see Who you really are and know what you really want, when you are all present and current and wholly Yourself. Seeming to yourself and others to be a part of the Universe, you intend that part; being all of it, you intend it all. Strictly speaking, will is indivisible, and it is all yours. Your will up against my will, ours against theirs — all this is playing the game of narrow-mindedness, mere willfulness. As the One you really are you really will, and you get what you really want.

To come down to earth again, you and I want to win. At least those of us who are at all alive and well, and sufficiently honest with ourselves, have to admit that it's success that we crave — whether that success is material or psychological or spiritual. But honesty also compels us to add that this is by no means the whole truth. There's something in us that does *not* want more possessions, power, reputation, creativity, sanctity, or whatever, without limit. In fact (absurdly self-contradicting creatures that we are) we discover sooner or later that we also crave the opposite of all this — less and less instead of more and more. Hiddenly we yearn to be relieved of all these mounting goods and the responsibilities and anxieties that come with them. Our achievements and acquisitions become fetters that increasingly restrict our movement, burdens that increasingly weigh us down, but we make little effort to break free. Addicts, gluttons for punishment, we are all too apt to go on clutching at more and more. Increasingly we are torn apart inside. A civil war is going on, with no prospect of peace in sight.

Peace will not come by moderating the conflict or declaring some kind of armistice, but only by seeing the conflict through to the very end — to total victory for *both* sides! Our urge to grow will never be satisfied till we become All, and our urge to ungrow will never be satisfied till we become Nothing. And— happy outcome! — it turns out that these opposite goals suddenly merge into one goal, a goal that is moreover already achieved. Here extremes meet and merge, and our ever-present Nature is Nothing-Everything. Our trouble wasn't the growth-ungrowth contradiction, but our failure to see it through to the limit where it is suddenly and absolutely resolved. Here at last our very own joy is discovered waiting patiently for us, because here we have what we really wanted all along. We wanted Everything and we wanted Nothing, and that's precisely what we have. How blessed we are when we let ourselves go!

With one voice the world's saints and sages and seers confirm this precious truth. "His will is our peace," says Dante. Conversely, our will — our willfulness as particular humans — is what shatters our peace. It is precisely what, according to William Law, separates us from God. Here is De Caussade again, "It is by being united to the will of God that we enjoy and possess Him, and it is delusion to seek this divine possession by any other means." A skeptical disciple of Nisargadatta's remarked that, if he the disciple were Who the sage said he was, why, then he could have anything he wanted. To which Nisargadatta readily agreed: "All will happen as you want, *provided you really want it.*"

But it's no good just taking anyone else's word for it. Your own oft-repeated experience of how life treats you provides the clinching evidence. Think of one of your notable successes. Yes, of course there was some joy at the time, but how long did it last? Has the long-term result come up to your expectations? Is it free from suffering? Alexander the Great didn't spend long relishing his conquest of the known world: he wept, because there were no more countries to conquer. The cynics who assure us that nothing fails like success are right — up to a point. That point is complete success, the success which alone is real and entirely satisfying. When at last we have the grace and the good sense to say YES to all those mixtures of success and failure that have been ours, the willingness to concur in everything that life is now dishing up for us, then a quite unique happiness, a peace like no other steals over us. Whenever we wish for what we are getting, our heart says we have wished well and made the right choice. This is what we really, really want. We have raised it to consciousness. This alone is true success.

The price of saying *no* to what we are getting can be very high. Depression and exaggerated anxieties and irrational fears, along with their bodily counterparts, are danger signals indicating that an enlargement of consciousness is required. These neurotic symptoms arise from concealed inner conflict, from unrecognized and unexpressed wishes that are incompatible with our surface intentions. We repress these unconscious desires which nevertheless belong to our totality, and which stand ready to compensate for the one-sideness of the conscious mind. For the unconscious isn't the monster which some take it to be. "Such a view," says Carl Jung, "arises from fear of nature and life as it actually is ... The unconscious is dangerous only when our conscious attitude towards it becomes hopelessly false. And this danger grows in the measure that we practice repression. But as soon as the patient begins to assimilate the contents that were previously unconscious, the danger from the unconscious diminishes. As the process of assimilation goes on, it puts an end to the dissociation of the personality and to the anxiety that attends and inspires the separation of the two realms of the psyche."

These well-known and widely accepted principles apply to what we may call the third realm beyond the psyche, to the realm of our third-level wish that everything shall be as it is. Just as our acute symptoms arise from the repression of our second-level and still human desires, so our chronic "existential" symptoms arise from the repression of this truly divine and basic desire. These "existential" symptoms are a glo-

bal sadness, resentment aimed at nothing in particular, a deep dissat-
isfaction with life as it is, a wanting that doesn't know what it wants.
Our cure is to shine the light of consciousness upon the deepest level
of all, upon the ineffable Core itself, our Source and True Nature.
There's no other relief from our deep suffering. We are well when we
know what we want. And we know what we want because we know Who
we are — namely the One who wants nothing and has everything.

And then we are clean out of hell and into heaven. "For there is no
hell but where the will of the creature is turned from God, nor any
heaven but where the will of the creature worketh with God." William
Law, again.

The foregoing is rather abstract and generalized, so let's give it
substance by ending this chapter as it began, with a tale.

Elsie had a beautiful voice and ambitions to become a singing star.
She tried and tried to get a studio audition, and at last — to her delight — succeeded. Then everything went wrong. She had great difficulty in finding the studio and turned up late. Another date was fixed,
but this time she developed a last-minute attack of laryngitis which
ruined her performance. On the third and last occasion there was a
mix-up about the songs she was going to sing: the accompanist took
along the wrong music. This was too much! She grew depressed and
nervous, and her behavior became erratic. Sensibly, she consulted a
psychiatrist. With his help she discovered that her deeper and unconscious wish was quite different from her superficial and conscious one.
She didn't want a show business career at all, but to marry and devote
herself to raising a family. Repressing her real desire, she was suffering
from the sort of symptoms that repression gives rise to. She herself,
without being aware of it, had cleverly fixed things so that the studio
audition never came off. And, as it turned out, this second and deeper
wish of hers didn't come off either. The possible husbands she fancied
didn't fancy her, and she disliked or quarreled with the men who did
make advances. Again, she made sure of failure, unconsciously. Again,
frustration bordering on desperation, and a new crop of psychoso-
matic symptoms, including migraine and ulcers. This time, however,
instead of going back to her psychiatrist, she went to a teacher who
helped her to probe still deeper. He got her to look at Who she really
was, and what that Who really wanted. She woke to the fact that her
third and bottom line wish wasn't that one day she should be a famous
singing star, or a happy wife and mother of three, or anything different

from what she already was. Already her deepest desire was realized. She knew that at root she was identical with all the prima donnas in the world, and that side of herself was already marvelously taken care of. And that all the children in the world — and all the grown-ups too — were her children. And so it transpired that the granting of this third and final wish of hers — that all should be as it is — satisfied her other wishes also.

Given a few adjustments in detail, Elsie's story is our own story, directly we care to make it ours, and to discover that His will is indeed our peace.

The above is a revised version of an article I wrote some eleven years ago. The revision has kept me busy over one of the most physically painful weeks of my life, during which — I have to confess — I have failed miserably to practice what I preach. If I have given the impression that severe bodily pain is easily accepted and borne, if only we unite our will with God's will, then I want emphatically to undo and withdraw that impression. Too eagerly I have taken on board De Caussade's "Holiness of heart is a simple *fiat*, a simple conformity of the will to God's will. What could be easier?" "What could be harder?" would, in the light of my recent experience, be much nearer the mark.

And yet De Caussade is perfectly right in this sense. I say YES to my *inability* to say yes to severe physical pain! After all, it is the will of God, alias my deepest will, that I should be no Stoic.

H O W
TO
S U R R E N D E R

Being united to the will of God you enjoy and possess Him.

It is in His purposes, hidden in the cloud of all that happens to you in the present moment, that you must rely. You will find it always surpasses your own wishes.

People who have abandoned themselves to God always lead mysterious lives and receive from Him exceptional and miraculous gifts by means of the most ordinary, natural, and chance experiences in which there appears to be nothing unusual.

— JEAN-PIERRE DE CAUSSADE

Inspiring words, coming from one of the great experts in self-surrender and abandonment to the will of God. But of course they are for testing, day in and day out, and not just for believing and taking on trust. And it's when we start trying them out in practice that we run up against what look like insuperable difficulties, some of which we address in this chapter. It is about practice and not theory. Here we are not concerned with the theology or philosophy of surrender to the Divine Providence, but with precisely how to give up and let be and let go, precisely how it is possible for you and me to arrive at and maintain this wonderful state.

It's not so easy to describe what surrender is, but we all know what it feels like — the sudden cessation of struggle, the end (for the time being) of all our resistance, the special sort of calm that follows the storm of what has become futile effort, the relaxation we enjoy when "something gives" at last after a long period of mounting tension and anxiety and all the fight goes out of us.

A beautiful presentation of this abrupt shift of mood — or rather reversal of mood — is to be found in Berlioz' overture *Les Francs Juges*. This celebrated piece of program music dramatizes the tale of a prisoner who is appearing on a capital charge before a secret medieval court. As he tries, with mounting desperation and terror, to defend himself, the music gets wilder and louder, more and more frenetic. Then quite suddenly, realizing that his fate is sealed, he abandons all hope and submits with perfect calm to the death sentence; and the music of struggle gives place to one of the great serene tunes of the world, smoothly flowing and even blissful. (Berlioz took the tune from a Russian folk song. In fact, it's common property, a perennial theme that crops up in unexpected places, for instance in the once-popular song *Now the Carnival is Over*, which is itself about a lover's resignation, if hardly his self-abandonment.)

We may take as typical our example of the prisoner on trial — typical of the dependence of surrender upon its opposite, without which it cannot exist. *Giving in* is as inseparable from *fighting* as *up* is from *down* and *left* is from *right*. You can't let go of something you weren't holding on to.

It follows that the mood of surrender can't be permanent: to be itself it must alternate with its opposite, with the mood of resistance. It's not in its nature to be steady. This is certainly common experience. We go on struggling against God's will as bodied forth in our circumstances, then somehow we find the grace to submit to it — for a while — and then the wretched process starts all over again. Surrender may come, but alas what comes goes. In common with all thoughts and feelings (no matter how profound or enlightened or even divine they may be) it is impermanent. Since it's a specific something with limited characteristics, it not only implies and needs its opposite, but is always tending to merge into it.

These obvious but neglected facts set limits to all *cultivation* of surrender — whether by reading and thinking about it, by trying somehow to work up the feeling, by various kinds of religious disciplines and practices, by any means whatsoever. The trouble with this highly desirable experience is that it fluctuates all the time, that it eludes our grasp, and is apt to be least available when most needed. Who, indeed, can feel *anything* to order? And in this instance there's something particularly self-defeating, and certainly ridiculous, about deliberately cultivating what must come naturally if it comes at all: about chasing stillness, about trying not to try, about holding on to letting go, about straining after relaxation. The sooner we surrender these absurd attempts to surrender, the better.

Is there then nothing we can do about the problem? Must we continue to let these alternating moods of struggle against the nature of things, and whole-hearted (or halfhearted) acceptance of even the worst of them, continue to structure our lives? Or, more likely, tear them apart?

No. The *direct* method of trying to gain control over our feelings proves self-defeating, but there is an *indirect* method which is more promising. The problem can be solved — though emphatically not at its own level or on its own terms — and solved absolutely.

The solution is ATTENTION, attention instead of intention. Attention to What is, in place of striving for what should be. Attention to how things already are, without any attempt to improve them. The fact is that total attention *is* surrender, and total surrender *is* attention.

Attention to precisely what? To what's given right where you are at this moment, regardless of other places and times. Just to read about this attention is no good at all. To get the point, dear Reader, look right now at what's taking in this line of print, at its Seer, its Reader — if any. Isn't it a fact that there's no-thing where you are, nothing but space for the scene (for a pair of hands holding an open book, surrounded by vague colored shapes) to happen in? Nothing where you are now but this speckless Awareness or Capacity, itself lacking all smell, taste, sound, color, opacity, movement, and therefore perfectly fitted to take in all these, and more? How marvelously accommodating you are!

This inseeing, this attention to What one always is, this discovery of What is beyond all improvement or deterioration (because there's nothing here to change or be changed) — *this alone is total surrender*. It is the giving up of every attribute and function that one had claimed, the end of all one's pretensions to be anything whatsoever. Not an atom of substance, not a twinge of feeling, not the shadow of a thought can survive in the rarefied atmosphere of the Center. Here remains only Attention, simple Awareness, pure Consciousness-of-consciousness without content or qualification, and This can never come or go. Here is Abandonment itself, including the abandonment of all time and change. One doesn't achieve this abandonment. One *is* it eternally.

All the same, this essential inseeing doesn't put an end to the parade of feelings and thoughts with their endless shifts and alternations, their built-in contradictions. Nor can it be counted on to "rectify" them. Maybe they will in some degree sort themselves out, and maybe the feeling of surrender will grow apace, now that all feelings are consciously experienced from their problem-free Source and Container right here. Nevertheless they remain in their own sphere essentially "problematical": it's their nature to be incomplete, in part false, at odds with one another. The real difference which this seeing-What-one-is makes, isn't the *improvement* of that scene (of one's thinking and feeling and behaving) but in its *placing*. It all belongs out there, in and to the world. What I used to call *my* thoughts and feelings are found to be thoughts and feelings about things there, not about Me here. The universe is as replete with sadness and joy, ugliness and beauty, fighting and giving up, with all the other opposites, as it is with color and shape and movement. All of it is brought to light by the Light here, the Light that is itself clean of every thing it shines on. You are that Light.

But you may object that this Seeing-Who-and-What-you-really-are doesn't last, that it comes and goes just as the feeling of surrender comes and goes, and perhaps is just as difficult to arrive at and maintain.

Well, try it, and you will find that, quite unlike the feeling, the seeing is always available. You can see perfectly well What and Who you really are, whatever your occupation or circumstances or mood. Nothing is easier or more natural.

Nor, strictly speaking, is it intermittent. It occurs out of time, inasmuch as it is seeing into the Place where nothing whatsoever — not even place and time — survives. This isn't theory for thinking about, but fact for testing. Look again and see the Emptiness that you are, and you will find that it doesn't read as beginning at such and such a time by the clock, and end so many seconds or minutes or hours later. I think you will find that it cannot be separated by any interval from other "occasions of seeing"', so called. As one of the Zen masters observes, "Seeing into nothingness — this is the true seeing, the *eternal* seeing."

Where there is no time there is no will or intention or choice: all three are time's offspring. Paradoxically, real surrender to the Divine Will isn't just giving up one's own personal will but all will, and resting in the perfection of what *is*. The only way to come to the place of no desire is to attend to it, and see that one has never been anywhere else. Right here at zero inches from oneself, at the very midpoint of one's universe, is the God who is the still point at the heart of the storm.

> We used to pray: "Thy will
> my Lord and God, be done."
> And lo! He has no will
> He is stillness alone.

So wrote Angelus Silesius, the Cherubinic Wanderer.

But in that case what are we to make of Dante's cry from the heart: "His will is our peace?"

The answer is to examine yet again the Spot one occupies and see how empty it is of all content of its own, and in particular of all will or intention. And see, too, how full it is of the scene, of the world as it is now given, complete with all the feelings and thoughts that are now coloring and enlivening it. Isn't it a fact, in your own experience at this moment as the will-less Source, that your will is perfectly embodied in what is now flowing from that Source, so that all of it is perfectly acceptable just as it is? Is it possible to see Who you are without endorsing things as they are? Is there any other way to true self-abandonment but falling into the arms of the One who is infinitely more you than you are yourself? The One who in Himself has no will, but is responsible for everything in the world? To see that you are not in the world, but that on the contrary the world is in you, is to be more than reconciled to its every manifestation.

First see What and Who you really, really, really are, establish your true identity, and then see whether you have anything whatsoever to complain of.

SIX SKETCHES
FOR A
PORTRAIT

The Tathagata divides his own body into innumerable bodies, and also integrates innumerable bodies into one body. Now he becomes cities, villages, houses ... Now he has a large body, now a small body.
—MAHAPARINIRVANA SUTRA

It so happens that you are, for the moment, something or other, some one or other. What's more, it so happens that you are able, if only you wish, to find what and who this something or someone is. If you are interested, you can do so now, easily. If it seems hard, that is because you don't want to make your own acquaintance. Not yet.

To waste such an opportunity (Can you be sure it will recur?) would be a pity. The Sages could be right when they promise infinite benefits to anyone who becomes truly self-aware. Once you dare look at yourself, they say, the rewards start coming in. Even common sense suggests that to know how to live it might be a good idea to know who is living. And plain curiosity or inquisitiveness adds that perhaps you had better take a quick look at yourself while you can, just in case you should be missing something interesting. Suppose you had till now been hoodwinked and, instead of being who you think you are, you were someone quite different — in fact the very *opposite* of all you had been so sure of! Now that would be a discovery indeed! Well, this is precisely the discovery I'm inviting you to make here. And I'm also inviting you to go on and realize that your self-ignorance, this astonishing blindness to what it's like right where you are, this case of mistaken identity, is the root of all your trouble and care. The only way to be at peace with yourself is to be at home with yourself.

I'm not asking you to believe a word of all this, but to test it, for yourself, as we go along.

There are many answers to the problem of your identity, but they boil down to these six:

1. You are what you think you are.
2. You are what others say you are.
3. You are what others see you are.
4. You are what you feel you are.
5. You are what you see you are.
6. You are what the Sages say you are.

Let us examine these six propositions in turn.

1. YOU ARE WHAT YOU THINK YOU ARE.

You think you are a human being called so and so, male or female, dark or fair, single or married, so many years old and so many feet and inches tall, weighing so many pounds, following such and such a calling, living at such and such an address, a citizen of such and such a country. You think that the description of you in your passport, with its photograph of a face that no one else has or had or will have, gives a fair account of you. You think you are really like that.

In fact, you identify with what distinguishes you from all others, what separates you from them. What unites you with them, the characteristics you share with them, you discount. They are not *you*. Insofar as this view of yourself remains unbalanced by other views, you are lonely, alienated, and well on the way to hell.

Now from where did you get this idea of yourself? From other people, from hearsay. You have picked it up from them over the years. And no wonder. Everyone around you confirms it all the while. Almost everything in human society implies it.

2. YOU ARE WHAT OTHERS SAY YOU ARE.

Your passport is for their information, not yours. Clearly they accept its story as the truth about you, and expect you to do so too. If you were to lose your memory and clean forgot who you were, they would be only too pleased to tell you. In fact, your parents, brothers and sisters, teachers, schoolmates, workmates, friends and enemies —all of them have made it their job to put and keep you in your place and prevent you from getting above yourself. Paying little attention to your conviction that you are somehow unique and of special importance, they have constantly reminded you of your human and personal limitations. Society's business is to point out — forcibly if necessary — that you are only one human being among millions, and must behave accordingly. And so you have come to know what people think of you. Now, sensibly, you take yourself at their estimate.

Not that there is anything wrong with this. It is a stage of your development that cannot be left out. Also it is the foundation of our common life. Society, with all its splendid gifts, is built on it. There is everything to be said in its favor — except that it is nonsense. A convenient and necessary nonsense, but nonsense all the same. This is all right, too — provided that, while you still have the chance, you see it for what it is. Namely, the very opposite of the truth about you. It is better not to be the victim of this huge confidence trick all your life.

3. YOU ARE WHAT OTHERS SEE YOU ARE.

In fact, if you press these other people hard enough, even they (or at least the more honest and observant ones) will have to admit that they were wrong about you. If you were to ask them, not what they think of you but what they actually observe you to be, they would have to tell a very different story, a more truthful and scientific one.

What are you seen to be? The man or woman in your passport photograph? There are three reasons why this won't do. Firstly, it's not what you are where you are, but what you look like some feet away, in another place altogether. Secondly, it's what you look like from a particular angle and under special conditions such as the lighting. And there are innumerable conditions and angles available. Thirdly, it's what you look like at a particular distance with the aid of particular instruments. And the instruments are many and the distances innumerable. If you are in any sense what you look like, then you are what you look like to all possible observers, whatever their optical or electronic equipment.

In practice, science firmly discounts the view of you as mere man, at a range of a few feet. It prefers the closer look. It insists on going into things more deeply and pushing its researches home. Approaching you, the observer discovers that the man is really an assemblage of organs and limbs, and each of these is really an assemblage of tiny living creatures called cells, and each cell is really an assemblage of nonliving things called molecules, and each molecule is an assemblage of virtually empty things called atoms, and so on through particles and quarks to the point of contact where you disappear altogether. It turns out that you yourself, at the Center and Source of all your regional appearances to others, are an Absentee, No-thing at all. This No-thingness is what you are where you are. All the other views of you were merely what you happened to look like from elsewhere.

Science is driven to take an ever closer view, with the idea of getting at the fundamental truth about you. But increasingly it is also driven in the opposite direction, to take an evermore distant view of you, with the idea of getting the whole of you into the picture. In other words, it recognizes that you as a man are a meaningless fragment, not all there and quite inexplicable till your world — till *the* world — is taken into account. In a sense you *are* all that you depend on: you are what makes you what you are. To be yourself you must be much more than yourself. Your physics and chemistry, your anatomy and physiology, your behavior and mind — these make no sense on their own. They only begin to make sense with the rest of you — your family and household, your suburb, your city, your country, the living Earth, the Solar System, our Galaxy, the Universe itself. Cut off from these, from your total Body, you are neither human, nor alive, nor existent. Only the whole of you is you, and the whole of you is the Whole.

In confirmation of all this we have only to see what you look like from increasing distances. Keeping steadily in view the Spot you seem to occupy, we find the human you giving place to the house, the suburb, the city, the country, the planet, the solar system, the galaxy, the Universe of galaxies. All very much as before.

This is the other pole of your being. Approaching you, we found you in the end to be Nothing; receding from you, we find you in the end to be All. Certainly there is something very special about the half-way view of you as human. But by itself it falls between two stools. It is neither close nor distant enough to reveal your true Nature. Exactly in the middle, it is as far away as it can be from the bipolar Reality that you are.

At this point you may object that these outside impressions are all very well, but what you really are is what you feel yourself to be, regardless of how you may look to others. Fair enough, but is there in fact any serious discrepancy between the two, between the outside story of what you look like and the inside story of what you feel like?

4. YOU ARE WHAT YOU FEEL YOU ARE.

What you feel you are depends on what you are up to. Infinitely elastic, you are as big or as small as the occasion requires. Intense sensual experience is the experience of some organ rather than the whole organism. You are reduced to that pleasure-saturated or pain-saturated piece of a human being. Out on the highway, on the other hand, you aren't reduced but much enlarged. You aren't a man or a woman sitting in a machine that is tearing along at 80 miles an hour. *You* are moving at that speed, in law and in fact and in feeling — all the ton of you. That's how you speak, and that's why your whole personality is so changed. You extend to your bumpers and wing mirrors and tire treads, treading the road surface. You are 6 feet wide and 15 feet long, hard, shining, beautiful, very powerful and dangerous, very impatient and critical of other cars, very sensitive about being passed, furious about every scratch on your paintwork. It is much the same whether you are flying the sky or sailing the sea. Suitably tooled-up and extended, you have grown the Body that fits your environment for the time being and your function in it. You feel yourself into each embodiment so naturally you don't notice it.

Again, when you read your newspaper's latest story of threats and aggression by *Them*, you think for and hate for and tremble for *Us*. You are identified with, you become *Us*. And *Us* may be a family, a social class, a nation, a race, a power-bloc, a planet ...

And perhaps, very occasionally, you enjoy moments of truly infinite expansion, when your heart goes out in love for everyone and everything, when you throw your arms so wide they embrace the whole world, and there remains not a dust-grain that is not forever You. Then at last you are Yourself, all there, complete. It's not that you feel *like* the Whole but *for* the Whole. You are just that. For only the Whole can feel Whole.

Such tremendous moments are not to be had at will. They come, if at all, by grace and quite unheralded. Much more familiar is the polar opposite of this mood of supreme exaltation, namely the mood of contraction or nullity, of depression to the point of annihilation. You feel that you have nothing, know nothing, can do nothing, are nothing.

And the remarkable thing about this feeling, when it is complete, is that it isn't a miserable one. Rather it is a feeling of total surrender and profound peace. For if you are Nothing, nothing can hurt or disturb you. Moreover, nothing remains to separate you from anyone or anything. All your resistance gone, you are ready to be invaded and taken over by your Source.

And if you should wonder whether these feelings — in particular the feelings of Nothingness and Allness — are reliable indications of who you are, you can easily check them by looking at yourself, for yourself. Looking to see.

5. YOU ARE WHAT YOU SEE YOU ARE.

You may object that you are badly placed to see yourself, that you are too close and standing in your own light. In fact, the reverse is the case. Only you are in a position to see and to say what it's like where you are, in the place you occupy at this present moment. All other observers are outsiders, off center, on business elsewhere, and therefore unqualified to report on you as you really are, right where you are. In the whole universe there is this one very special spot, this one very special occupant of that spot, which you and only you can observe. What does it look like right now? What do you make of yourself, on present evidence?

Do you see the head and shoulders figured in your passport? If not, do you see their contents, such as bones, brains, muscles, blood? If not, do you see cells, or molecules, or atoms, or particles? Isn't it a fact — the most evident and important and neglected of all the facts about you — that you see the *absence* of all these things, the total emptiness of the spot you occupy?

How can anyone *see* an absence? Very easily, as when you see the absence of fish and chips on your plate when you've finished eating them. In precisely the same way and — if anything — still more clearly, you can see that what figures in your passport photo is totally absent from this place where you had imagined it to be. Instead, filling the gap are two pages of this book, and two thumbs with parts of their hands, and glimpses perhaps of knees and shoes and a patch of carpet. Or else, it may be, glimpses of a window framing grass, trees, clouds, sun, and blue sky. Or whatever.

In short, you see that you are that marvelous Nothing which is space for Everything. Seeing this with the utmost brilliance and clarity

— and there's no other way to see it — you are fully enlightened as to your true Nature. That is to say, you are Enlightened. No longer in the dark about your identity. So say the great spiritual masters.

6. YOU ARE WHAT THE SAGES SAY YOU ARE.

The Sages say that you are quite different from what you think and what others think, and that your wildly mistaken estimate of yourself is the great hoodwink and the reason why you are miserable.

They say that the most direct way of dispelling this delusion is to reverse the arrow of your attention and look steadily within and take what you find.

They say that as soon as you do this you will see, suddenly and easily and to perfection, that you are Empty, Formless, Void.

They say that, directly you see your Emptiness, you will see it's Filling and how they come together in perfect unity. Because you are free of the world you are the world — a case of having your cake and eating it too. At last you see the world in all its splendor, because fundamentally you are uninvolved.

They say it will now be quite clear to you that your seeing and hearing aren't functions of your eyes and ears and brain — which you lack — but of the Void which replaces them. Thus emptied, you become what you see and hear. You don't detect it. You have nothing to detect it with.

They say that, seeing thus, you are Enlightened, which means you see through the illusion that you are a human body, or any sort of thing or object or substance.

They say that perfect peace, divine bliss, immortal life, total detachment, Buddhahood or Godhood, Liberation, Nirvana, are enjoyed the moment you see What and Who you are. And lost the moment you overlook it.

They say, and I say, that all you really need is a combination of curiosity and honesty about what it's like being you.

CONCLUSION

Our first version of your identity was that you are what *distinguishes* you from all others, what separates you from them. Our last and sixth version was that you are what *unites* you with all others, what makes you indistinguishable from them. Apart, these two views are the death of

IN
GOD'S
IMAGE

A small boy was drawing something with unusual care and concentration.

"What's that you are drawing?" asked his mother.

"God," he replied;

"You can't make a picture of God. Nobody knows what He looks like."

"They will when I've finished," came the confident reply.

He was serious about God. So am I. That is why I, too, have made many drawings of Him. Here is the latest of them. It is also a portrait of you and of me, who are made in His image.

Please examine this picture carefully, starting at the top and working down. You will see how it sets out the relationship between the many-leveled physical world, and humankind, and the particular human you see in your mirror, and the all-inclusive Consciousness whose name is I AM, and the Abyss of Unconsciousness from which that Self-originating One miraculously arises.

Where do I come into the picture?

I find myself permanently stationed at the midpoint of an onion-like (or, rather, half-an-onion-like) universe, at the core of its many layers or skins. Looking *up* from here, I find the outermost layers to be occupied, in turn, by such heavenly bodies as galaxies and stars and planets, including the Sun and the Moon. Looking *out* from here, I find the middle layers to be occupied, in turn, by such earthly bodies as clouds and mountains and hills and trees and houses (not shown in our picture) and also by humans, including the one in my mirror who I identify as Douglas Harding. There he is alongside other humans, the same way up as they are and, like them, furnished with two eyes in a head. Looking *down* from here, I find the innermost layers to be occupied, in turn, by my feet and my foreshortened legs and most of my foreshortened trunk. And I find the whole picture terminating at my Bottom Line, at this fuzzy but perfectly visible boundary drawn across my chest, in line with my outstretched arms. No sign of the neck and the head I was told I had right here. When, in the physical as well as the moral sense, I have the humility to bow before the evidence, before what's given up there and out there and down there — given to the headless one at the world's end — this is what I get. I'd better take notice.

Nor can this Self-portrait be dismissed as naive, as a subjective delusion. No, in essentials it's what any objective observer makes of me when he homes in on me, traveling through the onion of my appearances to what they are appearances of, to the Reality at their core. Starting light-years away, he comes to places where I'm revealed as something astronomical, then something geographical, then something human, then something cellular, then something molecular, and so on. Till, on arrival, he finds what I find here: namely Emptiness. And if he then turns round to look out with me instead of in at me, why again he finds what I find. The Emptiness is filled to capacity with that many-leveled scene, and moreover aware of Itself as No-thing and All-things.

When we were very young it was a wide, wide scene. As we grow older, however, we come to take a more restricted view. The angle of our tunnel vision may reduce to something like five degrees, on either side of which those increasingly vague objects are more or less ignored. We become wretchedly exclusive, self-occupied, narrow-minded and narrow-hearted, hemmed in. We become sick.

My own healing, which you are invited to try out and make yours — actively participating in it and not just reading about it — begins like this. I stretch out my arms at shoulder level to mark out that five-degree tunnel. Then, with great attention and continuing to look straight ahead, I slowly widen their angle till they almost vanish. Enjoying now something like 260-degree vision, I'm taking in and taking on the whole extent of my world as it currently presents itself. At once I experience an expansion, a vast breadth. What's so astonishing, what makes this breaking out — this cosmic flowering — so real and so refreshing is that my outstretched hands are for me as far apart as East and West. That's not how I imagine them: it's how they are presented. Visibly and truly I'm welcoming the world with open arms, actually embracing it. It's my world, and no longer alien. Insofar as I go on seeing clearly and steadily the huge scope of my embrace, the matching understanding and feeling naturally follow, and my acceptance of all things as they are becomes more and more heartfelt. From living a five-degree life I begin to live a 160-degree life. From saying "No, thank you!" and "Keep out!" to almost all the richness I'm given, I begin to say "Yes!" and "Come in: I've nothing to keep you out with!" In fact, I'm well on the way to loving the world wholeheartedly.

But I'm not yet whole, not all there. My completion, which is also the completion of my healing, is that I take in and take on the 200 degrees below my bottom line, and begin consciously to be an all-rounder, living a full 360-degree life about my true Center. In moment-to-moment practice this means turning the arrow of my attention simultaneously inwards as well as outwards. It means ceasing to overlook what I'm looking out of — namely, the Abyss, the Mystery, the unknowable but absolutely real Resource from which Consciousness and its objects continuously spring, without reason and without stint. Now at last I am well.

Such are the consequences of the shift from my false center over there in that mirror-man to my true Center right here where I AM. To the extent that I cease identifying with that headed and two-eyed and normal-way-up one, with his little arms embracing his little world, to that extent I come to identify with this headless and single-eyed and other-way-up one, with his great arms embracing his great world. The former is what, as third-person, I appear to be, what I look like to others over there at a distance, what they and their cameras make me out to be. The latter is what, as First Person, I AM: what I AM for myself right here and right now. It's the One I'm coming from, my Reality.

Our picture brings out the crucial and many-sided discrepancy between these two versions of myself. It shows how each reverses the other. In particular, it points to the contrast between their value judgements.

The right or dexter hand of that one over there in the mirror, holding positive values, corresponds to the left or sinister hand of the one here, holding negative values. In other words, what's labeled "good" by the former is labeled "bad" by the latter, and vice versa. For example, that one prizes power over others, success at their expense, the amassing of possessions, the knowing that crucifies mystery, and the so-called love that lays down conditions and makes demands: whereas this one prizes the exact opposite of these things. Our picture illustrates perfectly how that one in the mirror turns his back on the world and its trouble ("I've plenty of my own, thank you") whereas this one cannot turn his back but must face and embrace it all. The physical switchover from that peripheral one to this central one becomes a moral switchover.

Where and how, then, does God fit into the picture? He comes in at the Center, obviously. No other place will do. No other place is important enough and (on present inspection) vast enough and clear enough. If any doubts remain, the world's sages and seers confirm that, though He is nearer than near and His home is my heart's core, in the last resort there is nothing but Him. He *is* the picture.

For years and years I worked at an absurd and terribly self-defeating thing. Hallucinating like mad, I took that one over there in my mirror, the one whose face identifies him as Douglas Harding and just one particular human among myriads, and I turned Him round and brought Him here and sat Him down on the throne of God. Making Him the center of the world, I sought desperately to deify Him.

But it wasn't just foolishness and pride that drove me to this crazy attempt to be God on my own terms, on the cheap. I had reason. At one level I knew that to be saved I had to be Him. At a deeper level I knew that to be Him I had to pay a price that bankrupts me. For He is the one whose love is such that He takes on with His world all its suffering and guilt and darkness. He is the highest who comes down to become the lowest, and through self-giving rescues the world from itself and wins for it the joy that has no shadow. The joy that can be won no other way.

Our picture might have warned us of these stern facts. It features a fairly realistic impression of what crucifixion at the world's end is like, of how it looks to the crucified one. Here is our sobering reminder of what it costs to be made in God's image. "I am crucified with Christ," says St. Paul, "nevertheless I live. Yet not I, but Christ who lives in me." Who I really, really am, right here, is none other than the One who is love itself. No wonder, then, there's no healing my personal anguish till I assimilate it and take on board the anguish of His world.

How does all this work out in my everyday living? Exactly how does it enable me to cope with unlovable and hostile people? And with the world when it looks black, if not hateful? And with my work when I'm stuck, uninspired, bored, full of doubts? And with physical pain?

The answer to all such questions is one and the same. I admit I've no way of solving the problem at its own level, much less of rising above it. I find that the only real solution is to go deeper. Down and in and through. Down from that wholly unreliable and resourceless fellow in my mirror to the Bottom Line and World's End, to the wholly trustworthy One right here where there's nothing to go wrong, but only the Absolute Openness. And through Him to the Absolute Mystery. Down from that 160-degree world of things to the 200-degree No-thing that is their medicine and completion.

Not that I *talk* myself into this descent. I *see* my way through to where I AM. I see Myself here, and go on to love Myself here, and be Myself here, in the place I never really left. And this I do with the seeing of the One who sees, and the loving of the One who loves, and the being of the One who is. In short, I am truly blessed.

Dante was so right: "Blessedness comes from seeing: not from loving, which comes later." This blessedness-through-seeing is no vague or highfalutin godspeak. It reaches down and through the most earthy of the curved regions of my life. Not only is everyone I love, in the light of the Divine love at my center, loved better, but everything I do in that light is better done. To do a good job, see Who's doing it. The beatific vision is that practical.

I hear physicists nowadays talking about curved space and no longer about the force of gravity. The more massive the body the more it bends the surrounding space. Thus planet Earth, for instance, doesn't orbit the Sun because of the Sun's pull, but because she inhabits the curved planetary region of that very massive body. Her behavior is governed by the warp of the field she finds herself in, not by a tether called gravitation.

It's significant that this curved-space model fits neatly into our map of the First Person Singular. At the center of the map lurks the I AM that's aware of Itself as the No-thing that, abolishing distance, contains and indeed is All-things. As such it is infinitely massive, and accordingly bends each of its regions — ranging from the nearest region of particles to the furthest region of galaxies — to the appropriate curvature. Result: our nest of concentric circles, our onion or mandala pattern. How fitting it is that the science which is in the process of recognizing the crucial role of consciousness in the universe should (however inadvertently) start taking account of the way that universe is actually served up to the scientist himself as the space-bending First Person and never to the second or third person who, having no such power, is caught up in that bending!

There is no consciousness apart from the First Person who is always Central and Singular and enjoys the God's-Eye view of His universe, His image. Which is also my image.

And yours, of course, as that unique First Person whose name is I AM.

A JESUS
FOR OUR
TIME

The lost *Gospel according to Thomas,* discovered "by accident" in an Egyptian cave in 1945, couldn't have appeared at a more opportune moment in history, or with a message that speaks more directly to our condition and needs. In this early apocryphal Christian text, the living voice of Jesus comes down to us directly, bypassing all that men have been saying about him and doing in his name. It comes across distinctly, high above the confused roar of two millennia of Christendom, so-called. It's as if he himself had planted this beneficent time bomb in the cave at Nag Hammadi, carefully setting the fuse to delay its explosion till the world would be ready for the impact. It's as if, so tragically far ahead of his own time, he knew when significant numbers of quite ordinary men and women (as distinct from highly specialized and disciplined saints and sages and seers) would at last be capable of catching up with his vision of the Light, his experience of what he calls the Kingdom.

I can't do better than begin by citing a number of typical sayings, or *logia,* from this Gospel:

- Let him who seeks not cease till he finds. And when he finds he will be astonished, and when he is astonished he will marvel, and will be king over all.
- You examine the face of heaven and earth, but you don't know what's where you are. And you ignore the present moment.
- The old man will not hesitate to ask the infant of

seven days about the place of life, and he will live.

- The heavens will fold and the earth before your eyes, but he who lives from the One will experience neither death nor fear.
- Many stand before the door, but it is the Alone who enters the bridechamber.
- I am the Light which is over everything. I am the All. From me the All has gone forth, and to me the All has returned. Split the wood and I am there. Lift the stone and you will find me.
- He who knows everything except himself, lacks everything.
- We come from the Light, from the place where the Light comes into existence through itself alone.
- I stood in the middle of the world and I appeared to them in the flesh. I found them all drunk. I found none that were thirsty. And my soul was troubled for the children of men, for they are blind in their hearts, and they do not see that they came empty into the world.
- There is a Light in the Light-man and it lights up the whole world.

This fifth Gospel, or *God-spell,* is very different from the four canonical Gospels. It is a collection of the sayings or *logia* of Jesus, some of which echo his sayings in the other gospels, and some of which are unique to *Thomas.* It contains no miracles or tall stories, no walkings on the water, no raisings from the dead, no immaculate conceptions or ascensions into heaven or descents into hell: nothing at all to strain our credulity. Certainly it's a later compilation than the canonical four. Nevertheless some scholars believe it may draw on earlier sources than they do, and therefore offers us what might be called a de-mythologized Jesus. Be that as it may, the question before us now is the value and truth of these sayings, no matter how authentic they are historically, how far they are the words of Jesus, or of his followers and interpreters.

The Gospel begins with a warning, a challenge, and a huge promise. The warning is that these sayings of Jesus aren't just for reading. There's work to do on them. Their significance doesn't lie on their surface, their secret has to be dug into and exposed. The challenge is to persist in this work till the secret meaning is secret no longer, but obvious. And the reward for making this discovery is nothing less than eternal life and kingship.

Thus encouraged let's get down to work at once. If we are in earnest about it we are at once faced with some practical questions about how to proceed — questions of where, and how, and what. Exactly where are we to look for this good news, this treasure of treasures of treasures? Exactly how shall we seek it, in what spirit shall we address this most promising of searches? By what marks shall we recognize it when we have found it?

Happily our Gospel itself answers these procedural questions for us. It hands us a great bunch of keys for unlocking the treasury.

First take the question of *where* the saving truth, the secret of secrets, is to be found. The answer leaves no room for doubt. The kingdom — the place of Life, of Knowledge, of Rest — isn't above or beyond or beneath. It is within. It is right where I am at this moment, nearer to me than myself, than anything else. It is the Home I never really left, the focus and midpoint of what is at once *my* world and *the* world, forever here and never there. Which can only mean that all books — including, of course the one you are now reading, and indeed the *Gospel of Thomas* itself — are literally beside the point by some 12 inches. Out there, they are of no value except as pointers to their Reader, to the one who is zero inches from himself or herself. In effect, Jesus insists that you turn your attention round 180 degrees and simultaneously look at what you are looking out of and what you are looking at. It's as simple as that, and as easy as winking, if only we will cease pretending it's complicated and difficult and reserved for very special people. Whoever you are and just as you are, it is here, and here alone, that you will find the Pearl, the buried Treasure, the Deathless, the Kingship that is your very own. Here at Center, you are the key, you are the secret of these sayings of Jesus.

The second question that our Gospel poses is how we are to go about looking for the Treasure. In what manner and what spirit shall we undertake this great work that is really so effortless, if we are to succeed? Again, our text is quite definite. We must come to this adventure with inspired naiveté, in the direct and accepting spirit of a child, even of an infant. The Kingdom is invisible to grown-ups, as such. We have to be unprejudiced and attentive enough to set aside what we think we know and start looking all over again, as if we had never looked before, and trusting what we find. In this investigation our learning, our belief systems, our religious formulae, our common sense (so-called), our tangled web of opinions — all these are so many layers of a cataract blinding us to what is quite obvious to the clear eye of the young child. In other words, what we have to do is set up shop trading concepts for percepts, and make our fortune.

The third question asks *what* exactly it is that we are seeking. How shall we recognize this Kingdom when we come to its frontier? How shall we be sure it's our Homeland? What is the climate, the distinctive topography, of this Promised Land? By what signs shall we know that we have unearthed the real secret of *Thomas*, and not just some notion we have of it? Well, the clues — metaphors and similes and straight descriptions — scattered throughout our text are plentiful, varied, homely, telling, and often beautiful. This Dear Country of ours, our native Land, is a place of paradox and profound mystery, yet its air is clearer than broad daylight, and broader than the widest sky. According to *Thomas* it is empty yet full of the All. Empty for filling with whatever happens to be on offer, we might say. It is where the opposites — inside and outside, up and down, male and female (to name but a few) — come together and are one and the same. Here is the One not born of woman, whom no eye sees or ear hears or hand touches. Here is the Being of all beings, that remains when all beings pass away. Here is the Stillness in which all moves are made. Here is the Light within the Light-man that lights up the whole world. Thus speaks the Jesus for our time.

And now you and I know precisely *where* to look, and precisely *how* to look, and precisely *what* we are looking for, there's only one thing left to do — and that's LOOK. You look for your Self, I look for my Self, as if for the very first time. Yes, please do so at this very moment, without putting this book down. Dare to look at the very spot you occupy and see whether it is in fact occupied — stuffed full of anatomy — or, as Jesus says, empty. Empty, just now, for these printed words. Why not stop being eccentric and out on a limb — to say nothing of out to lunch? Why not be where you alone are and where you are Alone, the sole discoverer of and the sole expert on and the sole resident in this Place of places? The solitary Columbus of this Ever-new-World — the Kingdom Within, your kingdom?

Jesus had a rough passage. It was no joke to be so ahead of his time and place. How can we make amends? I remember a couple of lines of a hymn we used to sing as small children:

> What can we do for Jesus' sake,
> Who is so high and good and great?

Well, there's one thing we adults can do right away, so that his labor and agony shall not be in vain, and that is — not to believe this teaching of his in *Thomas*, but to test it, sincerely verifying (and falsifying) the scriptures by our experience instead of our experience by the scriptures. For instance, he tells us:

> If those who guide you say to you
>   "Lo, the Kingdom is in heaven,"
> Then the birds of heaven will get there before you.
> If they say to you
>   "It is in the sea,"
> Then the fish will get there before you.
> But the Kingdom is within you.

Dear Reader, if not for love of Jesus then out of respect for him, or out of interest in what he alleges you really are, or at least out of a blend of courtesy and curiosity, look and see if he knows what he's talking about. Put his words to the test by carrying out the following simple experiment. Just reading my words is worse than useless.

Point *up* to the sky now and perhaps birds flying. Or, if you are indoors, point up to the ceiling, and observe that your finger is pointing at something or other, and certainly not at the emptiness which is the Kingdom. Next, point *outwards* to those hills and trees and houses, or at the wall and door and furniture on the opposite side of the room, and notice that you are pointing at a collection of distant objects. Next, point at the ground or the floor. And then, slowly and with great attention, at your feet, then your lap, then your trunk, and note how in every case this thing you call your finger is indicating another thing, and there's a distance between them. And certainly, once more, the Kingdom is neither a thing nor distant from anything: on the contrary, it's all-inclusive. Finally, point to your "face". Now what, *on present evidence*, is that finger pointing at?

Is it pointing at a smallish, opaque, colored, textured, moving, complex, clearly outlined thing? Or at an Emptiness which, though packed with all classes of things and qualities, is in a class by itself, is quite unique? Look for yourself! Isn't it immense, transparent, colorless and textureless, still, simple, plain in both senses — and keenly aware of itself as all this? Going by what's given, dropping imagination, importing into the situation nothing foreign to it, are you not at this moment Capacity or Space for the whole scene, from sky to Earth, from Earth to feet, from feet to neckline — Aware Space for it all to happen in? I'm in no position to tell you what it's like being you at this moment. Only you can say. Please go on looking at what that finger is pointing at, and make up your mind on this essential subject — which is yourself as Subject — once and for all.

Surely the good news is true, and the Kingdom is indeed within you.

In another Logion of our Gospel, Jesus sadly complains that humans are drunk, are so blind drunk that they can't see their Emptiness. You and I, at least, have sobered up enough now to notice that we don't live inside small, tightly packed boxes, peeking out of the dark and sticky interior through two tiny holes at a distant world. No, we are out, out and about, up and away. Clearly we see how wide open we are, openness itself, at large, huge, extending right up to and embracing the Sun and stars. How refreshing, how liberating it is to be a small lit-up thing no longer, but instead the Light that lights all the things in the world. And this shining Immensity that you really are — how could this be born of any earthly mother, or (for that matter) be born at all? Is this the sort of thing that any funeral director could handle, or that requires his services? You who consider such questions are their answer. You know, you see, you are the secret of the *Gospel of Thomas*. Baffling you and me with no fairy tales, going easy on religious controversy and pious propaganda, it demands that we take nothing on trust. But try it out, and at once it makes perfect sense. It lays bare our splendor, and shows us how to live.

Running counter to the resurgence of fundamentalism (what a misnomer!) and superstition of every kind, a great simplification is going on. It is a movement away from the outward forms of religion — from their magical observances, their dogmas as incredible as they are ingenious (but still cruelly divisive), from massive ecclesiastical machinery creaking and stalling — a movement, away from all this obfuscation, towards the beatific vision that lurks at the core of the great religious traditions, towards the simple, patient, strongly beating heart of them all. Here is a transparently honest and antisectarian spirituality founded on direct experience instead of dogma and hearsay.

I suggest that it's no accident that the cave in Nag Hammadi held onto its treasure for some seventeen hundred years, and only gave it up when men and women had — in sufficient numbers to change history — become skeptical and sober enough to crack its secret code, revealing what is, after all, perfectly obvious. In any case, thanks partly to the Jesus of *Thomas*, it's becoming more and more difficult to deny that we are the very opposite of the little, opaque, unluminous perishers we appear to be.

The cat is out of the bag. The saving truth is the most open of secrets. The Kingdom has come, and the people are beginning to notice it.

THE
UNIVERSE
ENLIGHTENED

Your Self-awareness has wide implications and impressive consequences. It is truly explosive. When you see how vastly different
you are from what you had been told, you begin to see how vastly
different your world is also. You and your universe are inseparable,
and it must follow that, to be at all real, your enlightenment is necessarily suprapersonal and indeed cosmic. The tradition that the
Buddha's enlightenment meant the enlightenment of all creatures has
a sound foundation. It is as true of your awakening and mine as it was
of his. To wake up is to wake the world up.

What, then, is our universe like when, clearly seeing whose universe it is, we start living from that beatific vision? Does it make sense?
Is it a well-ordered and reasonable whole, or is it fantastic, the wild and
woolly product of the mystic's disordered imagination?

In this chapter I put it to you that, now you see who you really,
really are, your universe is much more reasonable and well-ordered
than it was. Moreover — to put it mildly — altogether more habitable
and lavishly furnished and welcoming, a home at once more homely
and more grand, more accessible and more astounding.

I have a further aim in what follows. It is to show that, even if one
isn't yet willing to see into one's true nature, the nature of the universe
is already revealed to any open-minded and thorough investigator. In
fact I would say to such a one: "As an encouragement and prelude to
"personal" enlightenment, try "cosmic" enlightenment. It may lead
you to conclude that they amount to the same thing."

Every age has its world picture, its taken-for-granted view of the universe and man's place in it. Ours is *supposed* to be based on science, and no longer on superstition or religion. But is it really the growth of science which has made a cosmology like Plato's or Shakespeare's incredible, and our own the only sensible one? Is our modern, educated layman's estimate of the universe really founded on facts or on prejudice?

It is certainly unlike the old estimate. Men used to think of the universe as full of life, of the Sun and stars and even the Earth as visible deities, and of the blue sky as the country of the blessed. Priests and astronomers pointed up to the same encircling heavens, to celestial realms whose divinity was proportional to their distance from man at their center. Physical height matched spiritual status.

All of this has now, we imagine, been finally disproved. Instead of a universe of concentric spheres we have a centerless one, a cosmic potato instead of a cosmic onion. Instead of an aristocratic universe we have a leveled-down one, whose principalities and powers have long ago lost their influence and their life. Instead of awesome star gods looking down on us we have so many firecrackers or blast furnaces blazing away in the night sky. Instead of a tremendously alive universe we have an inanimate one in which sentient beings, lost like the tiniest of needles in the vastest of haystacks, manage to scrape a brief living. Instead of a meaningful creation — a proper place for man — we have a huge expanse of mindless space in which living things are the rarest accidents or anomalies. And, in the last resort, even they are accidental collocations of molecules.

Such, more or less, is the new world myth. This is how most of us educated nonscientists — plus many or most scientists, in fact — regard the universe. And we are under the impression that science rules out any other view.

Does it do so?

First let us note that, truly speaking, there is nothing about the universe which forbids our taking this Earth — or the Sun, or our favorite star, or Number 10 Downing Street, or any other convenient spot — as its center. On the contrary, we have only to look to see that the *given* universe is always arranged as a nest of concentric regions — occupied by such things as pipe bowls and spectacle rims, hands and feet, people and animals, clouds and aircraft, Moon and Sun and stars — around the ever-central observer. To discount this eminently verifiable fact in favor of some theory (which is really no better than a convenient fiction) of uniform, potato-like space is in the truest sense unscientific, unrealistic, and therefore asking for trouble. If we are honest, the dead and centerlines cosmic potato is invariably found to be a cosmic onion, whose observer-core is the very focus of life and mind.

As for the outer layers of this onion-like universe, it is most improbable that they are lacking in life and mind. True, we have direct evidence of only one heavenly body — our own Planet. Nevertheless, according to recent scientific theories, a significant proportion of stars are likely to have developed into solar systems resembling our own. Furthermore, a significant proportion of those systems are likely to contain planets that are suitable homes for the living. And wherever the right conditions arise — the right ingredients and temperatures — there, scientists assure us, life will follow. Consequently the number and variety of inhabited worlds no doubt begs imagination.

It follows that we have much better reason than Shakespeare and Dante for feeling, on starlit nights, that we are gazing up into heavens replete with life, some of it far surpassing our own. To find the more superhuman of these inhabited worlds, we should need to probe further and further from our Earth-center. For the realm of the planets plainly holds far less promise (if any) than the remoter realm of the stars — the hundreds of millions of stars of our own Galaxy, containing who knows how many planet-encircled suns. Nor is this exalted realm a millionth part so rich in celestial probabilities as the still remoter realm of the galaxies, with its unthinkably great star population.

Thus science itself not only points to the existence of the superhuman, but links it with distance from ourselves. What's more, we are warned that the more advanced of the worlds above is likely to be influencing us all the while in unsuspected ways — say by telepathy. The laboratory evidence for this faculty is impressive: and, it seems distance is no bar to its operation.

In short, we are already back to something like the ancient world picture, which science was supposed to have destroyed once and for all. The joke — the irony — is that it is science itself that has led us back to that picture and done so much to verify (and, of course demystify) what was mere guesswork.

Clearly, then, we laypersons cannot claim the support of science for our pseudoscientific world picture as a vast haystack in which we are scarcely so much as needles. But consistency is not our strong point. For instance, we talk as if it were somehow to our discredit that our universe is on so splendid a scale, and as if we had lost instead of found ourselves in it. We think of ourselves as mere pinpoints in the universe, as if our inability to weigh more than one or 200 pounds apiece were somehow more significant than our ability to weigh the stars. Again, we speak of this vast expanse of mindless space as if it were anything but our life's source, saturated with and saturating our own mind if no other. As for the human self-portrait as "an accidental collocation of molecules," and one moreover that walks around blandly describing itself as such — now there's a delightful spectacle! If this is a sample of what our idiotic universe can throw off *accidentally* (whatever that could mean), think of what it could do if ever it got around, by some particularly happy accident, to doing it *intentionally*. And, in fact, we don't have to go far to find intention in what it does. It does *us*, who are bursting with intention. We certainly intend ourselves, and a good deal besides. And so, presumably, does every other star dweller who isn't on the point of suicide. How this universe can be so steeped in intention, yet remain merely accidental, we don't explain.

Evidently we science-invoking moderns think of "living matter" as if it were somehow freakish, irrelevant to the nature of the universe. Yet science insists that the physical ingredients of inert objects such as heavenly bodies are the same as the ingredients of the creatures that come to life on them, formed of their substance. The difference doesn't lie in the raw material, but in its organization. Thus the lowliest particles everywhere are capable of assuming the highest living forms. Potentially all the stuff of all the stars is alive, purposeful, and indeed superhuman. And even if such exalted functions were to emerge only for a moment in one spot, they would still reveal for all time the hidden nature of all matter. One small flower is enough to identify the biggest plant. There remains no sense whatsoever in our description of the universe as lifeless and mindless.

The scale of this gigantic thing is what tricks us. We are not deceived when we look at a creature of handy size. We take its whole life history into account, and most of all its later and more developed stages. Thus the plant is a *flowering* plant, even as a seedling. Thus the caterpillar is no mere worm on legs but a gorgeous butterfly in the making, even if it should perish before coming out in its true colors. *Flower* seeds, *mosquito* larvae, *human* embryos: the higher stages are always the definitive ones for us — provided our specimen weighs no more than a few hundred tons and survives no more than a few hundred years. Our unhappy cosmos lacks both qualifications. Because its scale is wrong its higher functions tell us nothing important about it. We see it as defunct, and only *infested* with life. No matter how unimaginably prolific it may be, no matter what myriads of living worlds and species and individuals our universe-tree may put forth, no matter how luxuriant its blossoms of mind and values (all arising naturally, we are told), we still reckon it a flowerless tree. Worse, it is no tree at all. It's not even a magnificent branching vase in which we, mere cut flowers, are tastefully displayed, but their indifferent or threatening background. Thus, idiotically, do we human flowers deny the life of our cosmic plant — because it's not *all* flowers, but also enormous leaves and stem and root.

The analogy is a misleading one. It doesn't go half far enough. You could say that a rose plucked from the bush is still a rose, but you must admit that a man plucked from the universe is an absurdity. Yet this absurdity lies at the very core of our modern myth, which sees man as his clue to what the universe is *not* like.

To say the least, then, the ancient notion of a living cosmos is neither ridiculous nor inconsistent with modern science. But whatever we think of the universe as a whole, the great majority of us are quite sure that none of its bigger parts is alive. The bulkiest organisms we recognize are the big trees of California and Oregon and the blue whale.

This is rather odd. For here we have, extending from particles and atoms and molecules and cells up to man who includes them all, a well-filled scale or hierarchy of unitary things or beings: and then, immeasurably above man, the Whole of things and the Being of beings. Why this cosmic gap? If the vast interval between man and his minutest particles is filled by a series of increasingly subhuman parts, surely the principle of Nature's continuity suggests that the equally vast interval between him and the Whole may well be filled by a series of increasingly superhuman wholes. If these have escaped our notice, couldn't that be because we have eyes only for our equals and subordinates in the hierarchy?

Have we ever looked for our superiors? Would we recognize them if we saw them? It is notoriously difficult to find a thing one has no idea of. So warned, let's assume that this gap in the natural order isn't empty. Let's posit a creature who outbulks a man as a man outbulks a cell, and ask how such a giant would have to differ from ourselves in order to live at all.

Apparently there are limits to the size of a terrestrial organism. If it is too big it is unlikely to survive. In that case we must assume that our hypothetical giant takes flight from his parent heavenly body and sets up as a heavenly body on his own account. Then he not only can be very massive, but needs to be. Otherwise, he can neither incorporate his own atmosphere and water supply, nor keep a firm gravitational hold on them. And without water and oxygen, and atmosphere shells to protect him from dangerous radiation, he cannot make the heavens his home. Nor, once there and thus enwrapped, can he just wander at will, but must attach himself to some star for warmth and energy, keeping a safe distance and turning continually, like meat on a spit, to avoid burning in front and freezing behind. And he's certainly a lucky giant. As soon as he starts spinning and circling round his star, the laws of gravity and inertia obligingly see that he goes on doing so without effort or deviation.

As for his physique, what would he want with legs or arms, hands or feet, or even wings? Nose and ears, a mouth with rows of teeth, a stomach and bowels and an anus — anything of the sort would be an encumbrance and laughingstock in the heavens. We are left, then, with a vast spherical body, its whole surface drinking in solar energy.

And supposing there was no convenient star to feed on? Well, if our heavenly giant cannot find what he needs he must be it. He must incorporate a starlike source of energy, a great blazing heart to sustain the physique we have described.

To sum up: if we greatly enlarge the creatures we know, adjusting their anatomy and behavior to their size and their very different environment, what do we get? We get creatures that are indistinguishable from the heavenly bodies we look up at. If our celestial giant and his fellows exist, they are a familiar sight, though unrecognizable at this distance. For all we know, many a star shining in the night sky could in fact be a tremendously alive and exalted being, a fit inhabitant of the heavens. And so the scale of creatures doesn't culminate in humans. The seeming gap is likely to arise from a defect in our vision rather than a defect in the cosmos.

This tale of heavenly giants isn't so much a fairy story as a detective story, the solution to which must wait till later in this chapter. Meanwhile, it's time we came down to Earth again, to the life we know for sure.

But do we know it? A living thing (scientists tell us) is an organization of nonliving things. The salts of our blood, the acid of our stomachs, and the calcium of our bones are clearly not alive, but neither are the atoms comprising our living cells. What is physics or chemistry at one observational level is a human being at another level, and at once alive and not alive. All depends on whether we take the thing to pieces or not.

But if the pieces, as pieces, are lifeless, where shall we set the boundaries of the living whole? If by the whole man we mean one who is independent and self-contained, we can hardly leave out the air in his lungs and the sweat on his brow — at least nobody has pointed out where these cease to be organism and start being environment. And if *they* are caught up in the living whole of him, why not the tools without which he would starve to death and the clothes without which he would freeze to death? After all, he is far more dependent on his shoes than his toenails, and upon his good false teeth than on his bad real ones. They have become part and parcel of his life.

That may not be how he describes them, but it's what they feel like. He identifies himself with his possessions and is not himself without them. He may be more vain of his facade than his face, and more hurt by the loss of a few tiles than many hairs. Until he feels himself so all-of-a-piece with the clothes he wears, and the horse he rides, and the financial or political power he wields, that they no longer seem outside him, he has still to learn their use. The expert is one who, having incorporated his tools, is unaware of them. They have temporarily vanished into his physique. He doesn't sit on a seat in a boat that sails the sea. *He* sails, *he* is at sea. He doesn't grasp a handle that holds a blade that cuts bread. *He* cuts bread. That's how a man speaks because that's what he is — an endlessly elastic organization of "dead" parts, mostly outside his skin. Thanks to them, he can drink at the lake and browse in the field while attending a concert on the far side of the Earth — all without setting foot outside his own front door. Instead of going out to these places, he grows up to them. In the well-developed citizen, the world's machinery springs to life and makes him what he is. These organs of his are all the more organic and lively because they are built, not of protoplasm but of all sorts of metals and plastics and so on, and can be amputated painlessly and at will when a new embodiment is needed.

Nor do these artificial but vital extensions complete his physique. Far from it. To cut a man off from his own and other species is homicide. You could say that a man is other men. And other species also. Species neither occur nor survive nor develop as separate entities, but in great interlocking patterns of mutual interdependence. Just as our own blood cells make no sense without our muscle cells and all the other kinds, so the bee's long tongue makes no sense without the flower's deep nectary. And so on indefinitely. The more you study one bit of life the more you must take the others into account, so that really to know one would be to know the lot. If, then, we seek the living whole, the Specimen that is truly self-contained and self-maintaining, nothing short of the entire network of terrestrial organisms, growing up as one living thing, deserves such title. And even this huge biosphere is still far from being complete. For without its core of rock and water and topsoil, and its envelope of air, it is as dead as the least of its ingredients.

In short, nothing less than the whole Earth is truly alive. Here indeed is a visible goddess. *One of the tribe of giants we were detecting in the heavens was down here with us all the while!*

Whose life is in doubt? Hers, or ours which is hers, or nothing? The only *complete* living organism of which we have direct and inside knowledge turns out to be a heavenly body — our Earth.

Of course the behavior and build of such a creature are, to our minds, so odd that we need a new word for this very high-level vitality, this superlife which is at least planetary. Oddity, however, must be expected here. The living cell is a very different story from one of its molecules, and a man from one of his cells. It would be strange if the living Earth were not, in turn, very different from her human and subhuman parts or organs.

All the same, she is no foreign body living some mysterious life apart from ours. Admittedly her life-preserving maneuvers in the sky are less varied than ours in her, but if to act deliberately is to know with scientific precision what you are doing and why, then her behavior is much more deliberate than any man's. She sees further and more clearly into her past and future than we could ever see into ours. Of course her beginnings were unconscious and unpromising, but so were ours, and now who can match her adult complexity — all her own unfolding and no invasion? For parent she has the Sun. For offspring, manned satellites and space probes. For eyes, observatories whose binocular (or rather multi-ocular) vision enables her to judge the distance of her companions in the sky more accurately than we can judge the distance of our companions on Earth. For special sense-organs, she has receptors tuned in to all sorts of cosmic influences. For intellectual exercise, her science of the heavens and her own constitution and behavior there. (I say *her* science, not *our* science, deliberately: here it is a planetary rather than a human function, and it is in our planetary rather than our human capacity that we engage in it. A human is much more and much less than human: all depends on what he is up to (or down to), on what company — superhuman, human, subhuman — he happens to be keeping.) We hang her portrait on our walls along with ours, and close-ups of her wrinkled face — ever-changing, luminous, with a beauty all her own — are familiar to all who take off from her surface.

This is indeed no alien godling. She is the full extent, the filled out body-mind of each of her creatures. For there's nowhere to live but the heavens, and no way to live there but hers.

To be more accurate, even she isn't suited to the hard climate of the skies. The smallest *complete* creature fit for this universe is no sunless planet but a star — a fully developed sun, a solar system whose "living" planet is a mere organ. And even such a star depends on all its fellows in our Galaxy, and on the Universe of galaxies. Only the Whole is a genuine whole, and therefore altogether alive.

So we have found what we were looking for — a superhuman hierarchy of wholes and parts to match the subhuman. Here, neatly filling the gap above man and counterbalancing the orders below him, are celestial beings — planetary, sidereal, and galactic — in which higher rank means more independence achieved and more "dead" material raised to life. And in truth all these hierarchical levels hang together, are totally interdependent. The life of man is the indivisible life of the entire hierarchy, or no life at all.

Is this view of man too speculative? Then let us imitate the scientist whose business is unprejudiced observation of what's on show (with a view to economical description and prediction and possible control). Let's try observing man objectively, for once. What precisely are you, when examined in this way?

What we make of you depends upon range. At 6 feet we see a human body, a little closer a face. But the superficial view isn't enough. Our instruments take us nearer and nearer, to places where we find tissues, cell groups, a cell in detail, giant molecules, and so on down to particles. So much for the near view. Let's now move away from you. This time we find, in turn, a house, a city, a country, a planet, a star (our solar system), a galaxy.

You may object that these objects are nothing like *you*. Of course (I reply) they are very different from the human you. But this is begging the question. We come to our investigation with an open mind about what you might be. We can only take what we find — namely, the whole scale of creatures from particles to galaxies. And this confirms our conclusion that you are incomplete, not yet yourself, till you are built to this awe-inspiring design.

Again, you may, with some show of reason, protest that the distant view includes so much that *isn't* you, provided you add that the near view excludes so much that *is* you, and that the middle view is altogether too superficial. But again this is question-begging. What are you, really, really? If our investigation is serious we can afford to ignore no view of our material. Only unprejudiced observation from every angle and every distance could reveal the astonishing totality and all its metamorphoses.

You might reply that this merging and emerging, this cosmic elasticity, however true of your bodily or outer aspect, is untrue of your "real self." Primarily you are a subject, not a mere object. And as such you find yourself to be "only human, after all."

To find out what's really going on, let's listen to this "real" self. You talk of *this* pore, *this* organ, *this* body of yours, *this* house, district, country, planet, star, galaxy. Clearly what is felt as *here* varies all the way from this aching tooth to the Milky Way, and what is felt as *there* varies all the way from all the other teeth in your head to all the other stars in the sky. "Here" and "there," "now" and "then," "fast" and "slow," "present" and "absent" — these little words are always giving us away. We would do well to listen to them and their message. Anyone who can seriously talk of near galaxies and the far side of the room, of old men in a new world, of giant atoms in a dwarf star, is either totally elastic or else beside himself.

Far from deceiving us here, language is only underlining the facts. A sick man may so identify himself with one organ of the body that the rest are treated as alien or even hostile. Conversely a healthy man may so identify himself with his family, or country, or planet, or even his star (witness the popularity of *Star Wars*), or his God, that he thinks for them, and is hurt when they are hurt, and makes their good his good, and lives and even dies for them with little thought for his private welfare. In fact, anyone who lacked all such expansive feelings would be an intellectual and moral imbecile. The idea of the self (I'm not referring to the One Self of all, our ultimate Identity, but to all the identities that fall short of it.) — the idea of the self as constant, as a unique, permanent, separate, immiscible something or other, won't bear examination. The facts — they include the evidence of multiple personality, religious conversion, amnesia, telepathy, and so on, not to mention the insoluble problem of biological individuality — make nonsense of the private and merely human self. Nor does this nonsensical idea work. Quite the contrary, it is madness. To the extent that we cut ourselves off from other selves we are out of our minds and dispirited.

The truth is that this illusion of a separate self and the illusion of a dead universe are halves of a whole, segments of one vicious circle. The universe seems dead because I seem out of it, and I seem out of it because the universe is dead. Till the total mind in man rejoins its own total body — the many-leveled universe — he is not himself and the universe is not itself. But when at last they coincide, this is at once his own enlightenment and the universe's enlightenment.

Short of that goal, his elastic mind matches his elastic body: *here* and *there* grow and shrink together, subject takes on the rank of object, you and I belong to the same hierarchical level. It is a human that greets a human, a ship that hails a ship, a star that signals (or tries to signal) a star. And just as it's not a hand that puts forth a hand to shake hands with you but this man who does so, so it's not a man or a country that puts forth a space-probe to study Mars, but Earth who does so. She is our astronomer — no mere man being equipped for the job — so that, in fact, there is the world of difference between the "I" in "I see a man" and the "I" in "I see Mars." Again, when the general (note the noun) says *he* will outflank the enemy, it is the army that does so. And when the atomic physicist (note the adjective) says *he* will smash the uranium nucleus, it is neutrons that do so. Yet he doesn't feel shrunken, any more than the general or the astronomer feel bloated. It comes so naturally to be at one moment tiny, and the next moment huge — to ascend and descend the cosmic hierarchy, taking shape as this member and then that, suddenly and at will — that we never notice the transformation.

To return to Earth, then, we have every reason to celebrate her life. It is an immensely important aspect of our own infinitely elastic life. But this leaves her peculiarly vulnerable. A word is enough to polish off this great but sensitive creature.

For we (I speak for the great majority of moderns) have only to decide, in the teeth of all the evidence, that she shall be a lifeless ball of rock, then no matter what limb she flourishes, or eye she opens, or *Song of the Earth* she sings — nothing she will ever get up to will persuade us she's alive and kicking. And why? Why because it's all, by definition, not hers. It's alive, and therefore alien or parasitic. Never shall the life *on* Earth be the life *of* Earth. How blind can we get? Treat ourselves thus, and what are we but cell-infested skeletons? Examine in this spirit the world's liveliest organism till we know it inside out, and we will find nothing but a patterning of particles. Earth is one of the most important and least recognized victims of our fatal habit of reductionism. Really it's time to admit that the most significant of geological specimens is the geologist.

And of course the Sun — come to life as our Solar System — gets the same raw deal. We have only to hand over the whole of his natural history to physics and astronomy (as if his men and beasts were unnatural and his flowers artificial) to reduce this star god to star dust.

A solar myth as curious as this doesn't spring up overnight. It, too, has a natural history.

To our early ancestors the Sun was simply alive, as you and I are, only brighter and more divine. But gradually the animating spirit was distinguished and divided from the gross body and turned into a god or angel steering the solar fireball from outside. Then science came along and reduced particular star spirits to general laws of Nature, to tendencies and forces. Till eventually, coming down to our own day, even these ghostly remnants are seen as man-made and subjective, and so exorcised. Heavenly bodies are no longer impelled or guided in their courses. They only take the line of least resistance. And while the solar life and mind are thus being wiped out, the body itself is being quietly carved up and disposed of. The Sun's color and brightness and warmth and beauty are drawn in from the observed object over there to the observing subject here, to the eye of the beholder. Even his apparent motion across the sky is really ours. Finally, and just in case any miserable remnant of our victim should remain, physics dissolves his substance into space, dotted here and there with inscrutable particles.

Here is the murder story of all time — nothing less than cosmicide committed over millenniums, and still going almost unnoticed. Fortunately, however, it's only a tale, a piece of solar crime fiction. For we could get rid of the solar life, by shoving it into our heads, only if our heads were lethal containers, or else made off with their contents to some other star. All that's happened, in fact, is that the life of our Sun has suffered an internal shift. It certainly hasn't gone. Quite the contrary. Doubtless it is only by thus shamming dead that a planet-ringed star can wake in the end to a fully self-conscious life and its full potential. After all, our pseudoscientific myth of a lifeless Sun must be seen as a solar rather than a merely human myth. As, in fact, a necessary stage in the natural history of our star, and no mere aberration. Only let's not mistake this brief (very brief, it's to be hoped) and somewhat crazy episode for the whole story.

And let's not mistake indifference to this story for neutrality. The universe which isn't seen as living is treated as dead. There's no halfway house, no sitting on the fence. We can't avoid taking sides. In practice, rejection of the ancient picture of a living universe amounts to acceptance of our modern picture of a virtually lifeless one, with its immense consequences for that cosmic anomaly called mankind.

To sum up, then. We have found our modern myth, this life-denying world picture that we imagined was scientific, to be nothing of the sort. Instead, we have found science pointing in the opposite direction, towards something like the old cosmic hierarchy culminating in the divine. To the onion universe instead of the potato universe.

The outcome for you and me is as far-reaching as we care to make it. Already we have seen that, once we breach the wall that parts our little selves from the hierarchy of our greater selves, the walls are apt to go on falling till we come up to the One Self of All. It's the first step that counts. Once we admit any life and mind above the merely human, we are likely to find ourselves admitting more and more, till we come to the highest Life, our total Mind, where we are safe, home at last and outside, no creature. Here we lose ourselves and find Ourself in a deathless world whose divisions and opacity have finally vanished, and where everything is indescribably weightless and open and brilliant.

To some of us this is danger signal enough. Our separate egos will defend themselves to the death. To others, here is a renewed invitation to the toughest and most adventurous adventure of them all, whose culmination is variously called awakening, liberation, enlightenment,

A GUIDED
TOUR OF
HEAVEN

L et me introduce myself. I am a travel agent, and I think you need a holiday. Well, I'm agent for what is the most exciting, delightful, fascinating, refreshing vacation of them all, and moreover one you can well afford. This brochure gives you all the necessary information.

No, I'm not joking, or pulling your leg. I couldn't be more serious. What's on offer is nothing less than a guided tour of Heaven itself. Satisfaction guaranteed, or your money back.

In all ages and lands people have believed that there's another land, a happy and healthy land which cures and reverses all the wretchedness in this one. There were two snags, however: visas were issued to very few applicants, and even they had to wait a lifetime for them.

I have wonderful news for you. These snags have now been overcome. Visas have been abolished, and this wonderful country lies wide open to all visitors, from one-day excursionists to immigrants. True, there are conditions of entry, but they are very easily complied with.

Of course all this seems too good to be true. Increasing numbers of people imagine that Heaven is a fictional wonderland like Utopia. Hardheaded, perhaps mockingly, they want to know in what direction this country lies, and how far away it is, and precisely what vehicles are lined up to take one there, and so on. To them I say: read this brochure carefully, and you will find clear answers to all your questions.

This tour has been set up to escort the members of the party to Heaven and, once there, to arrange an exploration of its topography and notable sights. To guide and encourage us on the spot there will be experts to point out what to look for. What we make of it all will, of course, be up to us.

I'll assume you have booked up for the tour.

It has five stages, which you should be quite clear about from the start.

First, you note and comply with the simple and far from onerous conditions of entry into Heaven. Next, you make the journey, by the vehicle of your choice. Then, having arrived on time (we make a point of punctuality), you look around and get to know every aspect of the place. Now comes the great moment of the tour. You, yes you personally, are invited to the palace to meet the King. Finally, you decide, in the light of all your impressions and discoveries, whether to put in for regular citizenship, or to return home for good. To those customers who elect to come back we shall be putting the question: "Is it really home that you come back to or is it mere lodgings, and is it really for good and not bad? What about booking up now for all our guided tours to Heaven?"

Let us go, in a little more detail, into these five stages.

CONDITIONS OF ENTRY

Strictly speaking, adults are not admitted. However, they are allowed in so long as they let go and revert to childhood. This is a necessary requirement. For until they can see what they see, instead of what grown-ups and their language tell them to see, Heaven is invisible to them. Heaven has no use for the intricate network of barricades and fences, set up back here by the Department of Social Make-believe and Convenient Fictions. All in Heaven must be free to follow whatever they find and in whatever direction, and to venture unrestricted all over the place.

All countries, of course, have rules about what you may and may not take into them — such as firearms. Some, Australia for instance, spray you before you are let in. The physical requirements for entry into Heaven are at once far more drastic and far less troublesome. You will find that all is taken care of at the frontier, so painlessly and so unobtrusively that you hardly notice what's happened to you. That discovery — and it's an astonishing one — occurs later in the tour program.

Let me assure you, however, that you will be welcomed into this country with open arms.

THE JOURNEY

This trip you are about to go on is as real, as *physical*, as any you have made in the whole of your life, and immeasurably the most important of them all. Accordingly it has a quite definite direction, or compass bearing of so many degrees. Let's settle the measurement, right now.

Point straight ahead. Keep on doing so.

You are now pointing in the direction of a certain country. (If you happen to be in the United States you are probably pointing towards Canada or Great Britain or Mexico or Japan. If you are in Europe you will probably be pointing at some neighboring European country. And so on.) But in what direction does Heaven lie? I will tell you precisely.

It lies in the opposite direction to your pointing finger. Its compass bearing is 180 degrees — not 170 or 190 but 180 degrees — from the direction that finger is indicating. Please then, with your other hand, point to Heaven.

All right, then, we know exactly where we are off to.

How far is the journey? That question, too, is readily and precisely answered.

How distant is that in-pointing finger from you? Look and see. I make it a little more than one foot, or 30 centimeters. Not a long journey, considering the exotic nature of the country — it's the true Wonderland — that lies at the end of it!

By what vehicle shall you make this remarkable journey? Well, we have some twenty available at present. Very varied in design, all are comfortable and trustworthy (see our other travel brochures for full details), but the handiest just now happens to be none other than that inward-pointing forefinger of yours. You shall be its driver. Please steer it slowly, with great attention, to the spot you are used to calling your face. All the way ...

Look for yourself. Here for the seeing is more than a glimpse of Heaven's spaciousness ...

An easy ride! And how long did it take to get all the way to Heaven? Three or four seconds, at most. Which compares very favorably with the performance of the latest spaceships, not to mention Concorde, on their journeys to lesser regions.

THE COUNTRY

Look for yourself. Here is the truly Big Country, compared with which all the others are tiny. One of the first things that visitors are likely to notice is that *visibly* this land goes on for ever and ever, and in fact has no boundaries whatsoever.

What makes it possible to be sure of this boundlessness is the perfect clarity of Heaven's air. There are no mists, no atmospheric veils obscuring far distances, none of the chiaroscuro that landscape painters aim at. No wonder Thomas A' Kempis calls Heaven "the Country of Everlasting Clearness!"

In fact, Heaven's terrain is so empty and bare that some who know it well have called it an immense desert. But don't let this put you off. It is equally true that the scenery is magnificent and much more varied than that of any other country — and this for a very simple reason. Let me put it like this. Heaven draws on and includes all the scenery of all the world. It opens the widest and most magical of casements on all Earth's countries. It's furnished with the frameless, glassless, speckless father and mother of all picture windows. People used to believe that Heaven looked *down on* the world, in both senses. Look for yourself. I think you will find that it *looks out at* the world. Already you can see, I guess, that the immense Emptiness indicated by your forefinger is chock-full of the scene, of the wall ahead, the furniture of the room, and so on.

And not only absolutely full of it but absolutely united to it. Far from standing aloof, Heaven so opens out to Earth that in a real sense Heaven is more Earth than Earth is Earth. I'll tell you why. Whereas Earth has no room for Heaven, and her inhabitants have no room for each other, Heaven finds endless room for Earth and all her creatures. On Earth, each observer, having split the world into two fragments — himself and what he observes — cannot see the world as it is. In Heaven there's no such split, and the world — now very different — is seen truly and as a whole. Heaven disappears in Earth's favor, gives its life for Earth, taking on every detail, however trivial or sordid. In Heaven you will find yourself so opened up, so built for loving that love comes naturally to you.

Many years ago, a client of ours made this sketch of his heavenly body:

Notice which way up it is, and what's missing. One name for it is our Resurrection Body. Yes, the old dogma of the resurrection of the body makes sense, but you have to be in Heaven to make sense of it.

There, you will find many ways in which your life as a heavenly body differs from the old life in the old country. Colors are liable to shine more brilliantly, shapes to come out more shapely, sounds and smells and tastes to sing ecstatically the praises of Heaven. But the most wonderful bonus is that, having died the death (without noticing it) at Heaven's frontier, you can never die again — decapitation being the most certain and summary of all the methods of execution.

Yes, as I said, there are certain prohibited imports into Heaven. And the chief of these is heads. You have to leave yours behind for cold storage at the customs barrier. Hence the saying in Heaven *Lose your head and find your heart*, or *Let your center of gravity descend into your heart and belly*.

Another strictly forbidden import is timepieces of any kind. Here's how the prohibition works: Hold your arm out there with your wrist-watch clearly in view. Look at that second hand ticking off the passage of time. Read what time it is out there, one foot from heaven. Now slowly bring it forward, and see what happens en route. Look for the moment when the watch shows no time, and the moment when the watch itself vanishes. So effective are Heaven's border regulations. Heaven is Now and timeless. Here you enjoy eternal life, instead of that endless future which is a meaningless dream, if not a nightmare.

In Heaven is perfect peace and rest. Not that it lacks the spectacle of every sort of movement. All of the motion and frantic commotion of the world is displayed in, and pivoted on, heaven's stillness. This, too, you can already see quite clearly, when you make that 30 centimeters journey Home, and start turning on the spot. Look and see that it's the world you came from, and not that Other World you have come to, that's whizzing round and round.

Well, I could go on and on. There are endless discoveries to be made in the Country of Everlasting Clearness. My purpose here is to whet your appetite for the feast that awaits you.

All these discoveries, however, are as nothing compared with their climax, which is your meeting with the King.

THE KING
About this meeting I shall not say much: it is essentially a personal

and private occasion. However, those who have enjoyed many audiences with His Majesty have left some hints of what goes on. They say that He is so gracious and so welcoming and so loving that it is more like the union of two beings than the meeting of two beings. Or rather, it's the heartfelt realization that, apart from the King who is Being itself, you have no being at all. Accordingly, He gives you a new name, your heavenly name which is none other than His name.

Heaven it is to be Him. No words can begin to describe the bliss of that ultimate identity.

This is for your encouragement, not for believing. Come to Heaven and test the truth of it.

I t ' s   U p   t o   Y o u

The fact is that, provided you did what I asked you to do and made those little excursions, you are up to it already. This brochure isn't, after all, an ordinary travel advertisement but one that includes a flying visit to the advertised destination. Overgenerous of us no doubt, but we think it's good for business. Before booking up for a tour, our clients have a pretty good idea of what they are in for.

My question to you is: have you had enough of this place, or do you want some more? Do your first impressions encourage you to make frequent visits, by means of a variety of vehicles to find out which you prefer? If so, we are at your service.

And, just in case you should be thinking of applying for citizenship of Heaven, let me assure you that this will not cut you off from Earth. Quite the contrary. As I said, Heaven is more Earth than Earth is Earth. The scenery of Heaven is Earth's scenery viewed as it really is. Which is to say, lit up and profoundly transformed in the Clear Light of Heaven.

PROSPERITY, ARCHITECTURE, AND COPING WITH THE UNEXPECTED

I was trained as an architect, and remained one up to retirement at sixty. Though the practice of architecture was virtually the sole source of my income throughout, it wasn't my real calling. My heart was never in it. By God's good grace and something like a forty-year miracle, I managed to hold down my job — in fact, to earn a quite respectable living at it — while devoting by far the greater part of my time and energy to His work.

There's no need to explain what that work is. Every chapter in this book is a version of that simple insight I go round the world sharing with all who are interested, and sit at home enjoying and brooding on and writing about.

I can't think of a more rewarding or intriguing job than this real one of mine. It takes me to five continents, and involves me intimately in large and small groups concerned with philosophy, psychology, religion, meditation, and the oddest mixtures of all four. As for the individuals I meet and work with — some of whom become very dear friends indeed — they run the gamut of the human condition. Yes it is, I can tell you, a life full of adventure and challenge, unpredictable, calculated to keep one on one's toes.

In this chapter I want to give two instances of this unpredictability, of the contretemps and crises that are always cropping up, and how they are coped with. True stories of how this man's extremity becomes God's opportunity, as the saying goes.

Two years ago I happened to be staying in Vancouver. Somewhat to my surprise I was invited to preach the sermon on Sunday morning at a place of worship I knew almost nothing about. All they told me was that the Church was "white" and "vaguely evangelical," and that the service was to be held in a hired hall and not in a regular church building. I envisaged a couple dozen elderly ladies in long, dark dresses — one of them playing a wheezy harmonium — in a species of tarted-up garden shed. Not a very promising prospect! But, as always, I accepted, on the you-never-know principle. At least I could talk about what I pleased.

Indeed you never know. The surprises that awaited me on arrival vividly reminded me of the necessity for open-mindedness and holding oneself in readiness for just about anything. The hall turned out to be as vast as a railway station, crowded and very noisy. On a large central platform various cheerleaders (that doesn't sound the right name for them) and singers, orchestrated by a remarkably ebullient and nattily-turned-out parson lady, were busy. I was led to a seat at the rear of the platform to await my turn.

The congregation were holding hands, stamping, swaying, clapping, and singing at the top of their voices. The lady parson was performing the improbable feat of conducting the hymn and leaping round the platform in what seemed to be a calculated ecstasy. The service (if that's what it was) must have been audible a block away.

Not my scene, I was saying to myself, sitting there. What had I to offer this excited crowd? What chance of calming them down till they were able to begin to take in my message? All I could do, when called on, would be to go blank, stand on my hind legs, and listen with interest to whatever happened to be coming out of the other end of me. I prayed — Oh how I prayed! — for guidance.

And guidance I got, with a vengeance. It couldn't have been more precise or more surprising. Not to say alarming.

The parson lady, having brought the song-and-dance routine to a rousing conclusion, and calmed down a little, called for testimonies from the floor. A young man promptly stood up and described how he had been threatened by an angry creditor who had lent him two hundred dollars. In his desperation he had prayed. And lo! a check for precisely that amount had turned up by the next post. He sat down, amid much cheering and handclapping. Several more testimonies followed, mostly financial but some medical, about answers to prayer. God was beginning to sound like a cross between a divine cash dispenser and an overworked medical practitioner.

And then the bombshell! The lady introduced me as the speaker of the morning, who would give an address on — PROSPERITY! Prosperity, I ask you. Prosperity of all subjects. Here was the very last topic I wanted to speak about. What I had to sell cost the customer the Earth, his very life. Poverty now — that would have been the ideal topic. Fondly, I had counted on being given a free hand to present my case, to share what I'm up to.

Well, here was this brother mounted on the high pulpit, his mind a Blank, waiting for the applause to die down, waiting to hear what would come out of the Blank.

After a long pause — I was beginning to wonder whether anything would emerge — I heard myself testifying that I, too, wanted to be solvent, prosperous, rich, very rich indeed. Happy-rich, not miserable-rich, or suicidal-rich, like so many of the billionaires and other hugely successful people one reads about. What's the use (I wanted to know) of the so-called prosperity that leaves one shrunken and bankrupt at heart? They tell me that the suicide rate tends to go *up* with the so-called standard of living. And yet, and yet — I still, like any other healthy human, want to be truly well off. How? That is the question.

There was a hush in that hall all right, and it didn't feel overfriendly. Unabashed, however, I found myself going on to say that, no matter how satisfactory our bank balance, or how valuable our portfolio of investments, all that's not so much as peanuts compared with the genuine, happiness-bestowing wealth that's there to be had, that's waiting and begging to be claimed. To go for that less-than-peanuts stuff amounts to sheer lack of enterprise, clear evidence of a mean and cheese-paring attitude to life. Truly speaking, the Rockefellers and Gettys of the world are improvident, penny-wise and pound-foolish. Poor tycoons! Who wants to start traveling along their road to their sort of prosperity?

No thank you! The sober truth is that there's only one who is rich, altogether rich, happy-rich. Not stinking rich but sweet-smelling rich. And that's the Creator, Proprietor, Sustainer, and Consummation of all things. The Earth is the Lord's, and the fullness thereof. In that case our best and indeed only hope of a little of His wealth rubbing off on us is to stay as near Him as we can. What about hitching our tiny wagon to His star, in the expectation of being occasionally spattered with stardust?

In fact, there's an infinitely more sure and straightforward and satisfying way of attaching myself to Him. *And that is to be Him.* To disappear in favor of the One who is more me than I am me. Do you talk of salvation here? Well, I say that to be saved is to be Him. Moreover, so far from this supreme Identity being an impossibly difficult attainment, it becomes the most obvious and natural state imaginable, once we turn our attention round and look within.

The deathly silence that greeted these pronouncements couldn't have been more eloquent. Among other things it said that I wasn't their favorite preacher, and would be unwise to count on many return invitations!

Of course I tried to assure them that all I had said was profoundly traditional, and indeed lay at the heart of all the world's great mystical teachings. Each of us is none other than the temple of the Living God. And of course — much more importantly — I urged the congregation to believe neither me nor the scriptures nor any hearsay but to test the truth for themselves of their truly glorious message. All they had to do (I assured them) was to take a look — aided by the in-pointing forefinger — at What they were looking out of. At their true Nature at core as Capacity, conscious Capacity for whatever happened to be on offer. As at once No-thing and Every-thing, and therefore absolutely poor and absolutely rich. Some in the front rows actually carried out this and other little experiments I begged them all to do. The rest, frozen rigid, sat and stared.

The silence as I returned to my seat at the back of the platform was deafening.

A collection, to which all were urged to contribute out of their prosperity, concluded the service.

It came to me as no great shock that I wasn't offered a cent out of that bulging collection bag towards my traveling expenses, or a cup of tea, or a word of thanks from that parson lady. She disappeared without trace over my horizon.

Nor was it astonishing to find waiting at the exit three shining strangers, who assured me with broad smiles and hugs that they had got the point, and what an Aladdin's cave I had opened out for them, and how their lives were sure to be changed from this moment on.

How untrusting and plain silly of me (I reflected) to imagine that I had been wasting my time and going out of my way to offend a lot of worthy citizens. What if only three out of three hundred had heard me? In this job of mine there's no point in counting heads. God has another mode of reckoning. Visible or invisible, His work never fails. God seeds had been sown in every heart in that hall. And, just as apple seeds grow up into apple trees, so God seeds grow up into God. There are no dud God seeds. Though they may be encysted and encapsulated for ages, they may be counted on to spring to life somehow, somewhere, somewhen.

In short, it wasn't an awkward situation that had been coped with somehow, but a splendid opportunity that had been seized.

My second example of how the unexpected crops up in my job, and how the worst can be turned to best account, happened in Honolulu. I was staying there with friends who had arranged a number of lecture-workshops for me in the city and countryside.

Duly turning up at one of the remoter of these events, I found some thirty people waiting eagerly. The chairperson introduced me most graciously as Mr. Harding, the British architect, who would address them, of course, on British architecture! Modern British Architecture.

Yes, there had been a monumental mix-up. What to do?

Three alternatives presented themselves. I could explain that, alas, I know little about how British architecture differs from that of other countries, and that architecture in general is no longer my field anyway. And go on to offer my abject apologies for the silly mistake that had occurred somewhere along the line, and make my getaway. The obvious, sensible course to take, you might suppose. Alternatively I could don the mask and bluff my way through what had to be the most incompetent and boring of lectures ever, on this or any other subject. Miserable for them, worse for me. Finally, a miracle could happen, and it would have to be no ordinary miracle. I could be shown a way of genuinely, and without the slightest compromise addressing at once the subject they had come to hear about, and the very different subject I had come to talk about. So that, in effect, the two subjects would turn out to be not so much contrasting as profoundly complementary, and both audience and speaker would be catered for. An impossible convergence, an almost unthinkable miracle, you would think.

And so thought I. In fact, I knew it.

And then I remembered that the great secret of life, the great know-how, is *not* to know, to be at a loss. To be, precisely, at my wit's end, which is the beginning of the Wit of the One I really, really am. How can He take over so long as I'm determined to hang on to little me?

Going quite blank, then, leaning back on the Resource that has never let me down, I heard myself addressing those Hawaiian friends roughly as follows:

I'll assume that, at the conclusion of this meeting, you will go back home to the house which, though similar to its neighbors, you unmistakably recognize as your own. Let me assume, too, that for once you linger at the garden gate, taking in (I hope approvingly and as if for the first time) your front elevation, noting the shape and number and arrangement of the windows, the front door, and so on. This is important, because it is the front you present to the world.

Examined from where you stand outside, and purely on present evidence, there's nothing to tell anybody what's inside. The curtains and the reflections in the glass prevent people seeing in. For all the outsider can tell to the contrary at this moment, the interior might be so stacked with crates of furniture that there's not an inch left in there for any occupier. "What interior?" one might well ask. In fact, *going only by what can actually be seen*, one might well be inspecting a solid object and not a hollow one.

"Enough of this nonsense!" I can hear you saying, "I don't need anybody to tell me to look within, I'm not a displaced person shut out of house and home. I belong in there." At once you dispel the last lurking doubt by walking down the garden path, unlocking the front door, and entering the spaciousness that is well-named your Living Room. Looking all around and making yourself comfortable in here, you can't help but notice how radically different the hollowed-out interior of your house is from the filled-out exterior, and how few and unreliable are the clues that the solid-looking front elevation gives to the space it encloses. Visitors to my own house back in England are frequently astonished at how deceptive the exterior is. The inside turns out to be so much more roomy than they had expected (In fact, my principal aim in designing the house had been — by means of strategically placed mirrors, corners you can't see round, and very open planning — to squeeze a quart out of a pint pot, as the saying goes.). And no wonder, of course, the outside of even the most standardized and conventional of houses is so different from — in important ways the very opposite of — its inside. Why? For the very simple reason that the former is for looking at while the latter is for looking out of. And because the business of the former is to enclose and wall-up space, while the business of the latter is to open up and open out space. The former provides a solid public facade for your private Living Room, while the latter provides that Living Room itself.

Of course it's true that the windows and doors that figure on your outside figure on your inside also. But just about there the similarity ends. The rest is contrast.

So far, all this may sound like painstaking detection of the obvious. I agree, but add that it's the obvious things about our life that are at once most overlooked and undervalued. Be patient with me while I continue for a little while in the same vein.

You discover, lurking in this house of yours, a mysterious stranger. A curiously self-contained stranger, housed inside premises of his own. A very snugly housed creature, somewhat along the lines of a snail or a tortoise. Whereas your outer carapace (of bricks and tiles and glass and so on) was hard and rigid and hairless, his ranges from tough to flabby and from smooth to hairy. He sports a front door that, instead of swinging, opens up and down in the manner of a castle's portcullis. And two tiny windows, one on either side of the portcullis, furnished with shutters that are closed at night and very frequently closed and opened during the day. As for the general shape of his housing, it's not rectilinear like yours but rounded like a snail's. His is a very different style of architecture indeed. You could call it Classic Curvaceous. Windows it has, and doors, and thatch of sorts, and columns and wings of sorts, and often is superbly beautiful.

There remain three outstanding differences. This creature's home builds and maintains and repairs itself from within. It's remarkably flexible. It is mobile. So much so that you could liken your house to a fancy garage for a camper-like occupant.

Just who is this energetic and beautiful stranger in your midst, this unbidden guest (surely not a parasite) who makes himself so free of your premises?

There's no point in keeping up the pretence any longer. Far from being a stranger, he's your personal embodiment, your own flesh and blood. It's his housing, his architecture, which we have briefly been examining from the far side of the room, just as we examined your bricks-and-mortar housing from the far side of the garden.

Need I say that it, too, has an inside, the place that portcullis door opens into, the place those two tiny windows are somehow lighting up? It, too, is for inhabiting. Obviously it, too, is for looking out of, and not just for looking at. You belong in there. You don't haunt your garden contemplating your bricks-and-mortar facade, neither — if you have any sense — do you haunt your Living Room contemplating your flesh-and-blood face. No, you move right in. You get the other side of that face. You take possession of your house-within-your-house, and are thus doubly housed. A very neat and desirable arrangement.

But wait a minute. *Do* you move in? Do you really and truly, do you *consciously*, take up residence? I wonder.

The amazing fact is that quite likely you do not. It's all too easy to put off, or delay indefinitely, the date of taking possession, on the vague and unexamined assumption that all those vividly illustrated wall charts and anatomy books (to say nothing of messages about autopsies conducted in morgues) reveal that this inner house of yours is bunged up solid with organs that leave no Living Room for you at all. It certainly looks as if your home base is so marvelously equipped with all the gadgetry you need or might need that you are crowded out, a species of displaced person living a literally eccentric life. The possibility that you, yes you as First Person Singular, are unique and not like any of those Second and Third Persons — that in startling contrast to them you are quite hollow and possessed of all the Living Room in the world — may well never have occurred to you. I'm going to assume that it hasn't. No disrespect to you. With rare exceptions, the universal human delusion — a belief so taken for granted that nobody thinks of spelling it out — is that physically (repeat physically) one is no different, as First Person Singular, from all the rest of the species. That, in short, one is as full of stuff as they are.

In the brief time that remains to me, I want to show how crazy this belief is. I want to lay before you, in outline, the evidence for your absolute uniqueness in all important respects, and in particular for the speckless immensity that awaits you in your house-within-your-house, and how easy it is to move in.

For clarity I split my argument into four sections:
1. Tradition
2. Look for Yourself
3. Homing
4. The Practical Test

1. TRADITION

The Perennial Philosophy — that's to say the great mystical traditions that lie, more or less concealed, at the heart of Hinduism, Buddhism, Taoism, Judaism, Christianity and Islam — agree on two basic propositions: (a) That withinside, at center and essentially, you are an immense Clarity that goes by many names, such as Spirit, Voidness, the Kingdom of Heaven, the Temple of God, Space, Transparency, Capacity, No-thing alive to itself as No-thing, Boundless Emptiness ... The terms are many and varied their import one and the same. Viewed from within (they say) you are wider and clearer and more open than the cloudless sky and (b) That your well-being consists in looking steadily within and being That which you see. To enjoy and consciously live from this vision of your True Nature is to be saved, liberated, enlightened, awakened. Saved from death and all evil, liberated from the chains that bound you, enlightened about your Identity, awakened from your long sleep. Again, the language differs from tradition to tradition, but the general import is the same. You had better look within and take seriously what you find, or else —

I think you will agree that a doctrine so universal and ancient, and now going stronger than ever, is unlikely to be a load of rubbish, mere wishful thinking with no foundation in fact. At the very least it demands to be tested as honestly and thoroughly as possible. If there's a hypothesis that begs for the most energetic examination, it is this, it is this.

The next step is obvious. Just take a look, right away, for yourself.

2. LOOK FOR YOURSELF

You dispelled those rather absurd lurking doubts about the Space or Living Room in your house by opening and walking in your front door. Now you repeat the exercise by opening and walking in the front door of your inner house. This you do by opening your mouth as wide as it will go, bringing up your in-pointing forefinger, poking it half an inch into the cavity, and keeping it there while you take stock of what it's pointing to.

I suggest that, provided you drop imagination and import nothing into the occasion that belongs to other occasions, you will find yourself pointing to an interior emptiness without content or boundaries. You don't think or feel this emptiness, you see this infinite Space which has not only dissolved your finger and most of your hand, but also every trace of that alleged anatomy of yours. On present evidence you are what the Perennial Philosophy says you are. The great tradition has got it exactly right. In that case, get the feel of Home, spread yourself, be the Boundless Emptiness. Start getting used to your True Nature.

I think I hear you complaining that, even if it happens to be true, this is unwelcome news. What could be duller and more boring than being Nothing Whatsoever, stuck forever in the place where Nothing Whatsoever happens?

Not to worry. This inner house of yours is not windowless, any more than it is doorless. Look and see. The two tiny windows that appear on the outside merge into one immense, glassless, frameless picture window commanding a spectacular view of the ever-changing world. In fact, so far from being *merely* empty and therefore excruciatingly depressing, your Space is filled to capacity with the scene — starting with bits and pieces of your curvaceous architecture (such as trunk and limbs), going on to bits and pieces of your rectilinear architecture (such as mats and walls and doors) and then the views framed by those windows. You could say that your Boundless Space is so saturated with the scene that they have become as inseparable as they are distinguishable. Or, as the Zen people put it, Nirvana (your No-thingness) *is* Samsara (your world of things, your Every-thingness), and vice versa. Or, as I would put it, you make the best of both worlds by being the one that's forever the same and having the one that's forever changing. You are one with the world, and safe from the world.

Don't believe a word of all this. See for yourself whether it's not perfectly obvious, once you look in the obvious place.

Only come to your senses, come home to the Home you never really left, cease playing the Displaced Person Game, and discover what it is to be truly blessed.

3. HOMING

Does it still strike you as both absurd and absurdly pretentious — this claim to be so grandly architected, to be hollowed-out and filled-in on such a scale and in such an extraordinary fashion? "What's so special about me?" you ask.

I'll tell you precisely.

You are for going all the way up to, and losing, and finding in your place the God who sees Himself as No-thing and Every-thing. That's what is so marvelously special about you. Others — bless their hearts — are for stopping short of. Viewing them from a distance, you find them to be limited things made up of limited things. This is no defect on their part. On the contrary, it's what makes them so valuable, so appealing, so precious. *Only you are for disappearing.*

Once you have the courage and the enterprise to move into your house-within-a-house, you will see how right the Holy Koran was to say that you are "like a mirage in the desert that the thirsty man takes to be water, until he comes up to it and finds it to be nothing, and where he thought it to be, there he finds God." And you couldn't be more special than that!

Range is what matters. Move in towards yourself, and you have a long succession of perishing appearances. Move all the way in, and you are the Imperishable Reality they are appearances of. If you want to be Yourself and no longer a shadow of Yourself, if you want to be Real, you must break the habit of continually leaping out of yourself in the effort to see yourself from out there as others see you, and cultivate the habit of sitting at Home and seeing yourself as you see yourself.

What a palace is then yours, and how perfectly architected for its royal occupant!

4. THE PRACTICAL TEST

I take your final query to run something like this: "How does this way of viewing one's life affect that life? If it's as true and important as you make out, the practical consequences must be impressive. To put it crudely, what payoff may I expect, in terms of everyday living, if I stop playing what you call the Displaced Person Game?"

I promise you that the rewards will be proportional to the seriousness and persistence of your Homecoming. But they will be unique to you, and I can't predict them in any detail. There are four things, however, that I can safely say:

1. The more you go for the real truth and the less for the rewards, the more rewards you will get.
2. You will tap new energies. This is because you are breaking the exhausting habit of eccentricity, and instead are tapping the Source of all energies within, at Center.
3. You will find yourself approaching the unself-consciousness and spontaneity that you enjoyed as a little child. With this difference: then you simply lived from your Home, now you do so with full awareness. But now, as then, you are Space for the people around you to occupy, and by no means one of them. The freedom, the

relief, is awesome. Specially if, like me, you had suffered excruciatingly from shame-facedness.

4.   In effect, you will perceive that you are *built for loving*. That's to say
     that, in your house-within-the-house you are Empty for the loved
     one. You vanish in favor of — you give your life for — that one.
     The feeling follows the vision. Your heart opens, your love starts to
     flow naturally and freely.

     Be patient. Don't demand that these or any other blessings
     will be apparent at once. Moving house takes time and attention.

In conclusion, let me speak quite frankly.

While handing you the key of your new home, the real estate agent
doesn't advise you to use it and venture inside. How unlike the realtor
who hands you the key of your home within your home. Along with all
the other agents and seers of Reality down the ages and speaking with
one voice, he implores you to look within. Why should he do that?
Because he has good reason for assuming that you are hellbent on
staying outside.

It's up to each one of you to prove him wrong.

That, as nearly as I can remember, was the substance of the talk on
Architecture that those Hawaiian friends listened to. Good-humoredly,
I must say. I think they got the impression that British architects are a
curious lot. Whether any of them were convinced that they were built
to the most open of plans, or built for loving and for giving one's life
for others, I doubt. All I can be sure of is that I learned a very great
deal from what had begun by looking like no more than a silly foul-up.
Once again, man's extremity had turned out to be God's opportunity.

I'm confident, in fact, that once you dedicate yourself to Homecoming, everything that happens to you is really refreshment and fuel
for that journey of journeys. The old hymn writer said a true thing:

> Ye fearful saints fresh courage take,
> The clouds ye so much dread
> Are big with mercy and shall break
> With blessings on your head.

A WALK
IN THE
FOREST

This summer, while walking in the tree-covered mountains of La Drôme, in the south of France, I made a curious discovery. Curious, and quite useful. Useful, at least, for elderly hikers like me.

The unpaved forest roads, with their easy gradients, were fairly good for walking, provided you were careful not to trip up over loose boulders, bits of projecting rock, and potholes. Aware of this danger, I paid close attention to the road surface, delicately picking my way among its obstacles and only occasionally stubbing a toe or twisting an ankle.

My caution worked fairly well, but it had two disadvantages: my walk in the forest became more like a totter in the forest, and I missed the forest. The wayside flowers (at their very best), the trees, the gaps in them revealing deep valleys and distant mountains — all these were more or less lost on me. My landscape was a pair of feet, uneasily negotiating miniature valleys and mountains.

I soon got tired of this monotonous scenery underfoot, and decided to try an altogether different way of walking. Taking (I thought) rather a risk, *I looked steadily ahead instead of down*. There in the middle distance rose the white, tree-bordered path, widening and blurring as it approached me, and finally vanishing altogether in me. No underfoot hazards now, no legs or feet to cope with them, nothing at all as near as that. It was as if the road right here were being rolled smooth enough for safe walking, and in fact rolled up altogether. If there remained anybody walking (which there didn't), he was walking on air.

No, I didn't fall flat on my face or sprain an ankle. Quite the contrary, I became remarkably sure-footed — because no-footed. And I was free to enjoy the forest and the distant views. The new method worked.

At least it worked so long as I didn't lose myself in that scene. It worked very well so long as I remained centered, aware of myself as the Space in which that ever-changing forest-scene was on display, aware of the Absence here of any walker in the forest, aware of the Nothing here that was making nothing of that difficult road surface. For I soon found that when something out there captivated me and I lost touch with my spaciousness here I started stumbling about again. It seemed that this central emptiness functioned best when it was keenly alive to itself as empty. It seemed that I had consciously to dissolve those approaching hazards and the feet and legs that had been trying so hard to cope with them. Otherwise they would begin tripping me up.

I remembered the sad story of the centipede who got around quite happily till some busybody asked him how he managed to control all those legs. What expertise, to coordinate so effectively all those moving parts! Poor centipede: one anxious glance down at the machinery of locomotion and it halted, never to move again.

There were unfamiliar butterflies at the roadside and swallows overhead. Everywhere such consummate skill in flight: the butterflies dodging this way and that to avoid capture, the swallows (perfect aviators from the start) making human aerobatics look graceless, amateurish, and very dangerous. Certainly no swallow looks back to monitor those incredibly fine adjustments to wings and tail in flight: one good look, and I guess the little creature would fall like a stone from the sky. *For itself*, no bird is a bird, no animal is an animal, and that is why it moves so beautifully for us. It *is* the scene ahead. Have you ever caught your cat looking down at its paws while walking, or tripping up over a dropped toy? Observe toddlers learning to walk. They lean forward, intent on what lies ahead, and leave their little legs to stagger along somehow behind. The truth (the first-person story) is that we learn to walk without legs, and only acquire such underpinning later in life. With what result? Watch young children at the seaside, running about on seaweed-covered and very slippery rocks, hardly ever glancing down yet hardly ever coming to grief: and compare their performance with their parents' painfully slow and unsteady footwork over the same terrain. It's as though they were walking on stilts for the first time.

How to regain this lost art of the young child, the cat, the swallow — the art of unhesitating and appropriate movement without attending to moving parts? There's no going back to Paradise and infancy. I can no longer simply give place to — make room for — those distant hills and trees. That scene is not enough to empty me of myself. Why? Because there persists the *idea* of something here (me) reacting to something there (not-me). The steady assumption of every grown-up, the basis of his life as a man among men (all the more massive for remaining unexamined) is that there lies at the center of his universe a solid, opaque, colored, complicated, active *thing*, mostly invisible to its owner but nevertheless perfectly real. This universal human conviction isn't spelled out in so many words. It doesn't need to be, it's too evident, it goes without saying. And it's a lie! Actually, it's *the* lie.

It's a lie that goes on repeating itself and building itself up till one fine day — if I'm lucky — it becomes so painful and embarrassing that I'm driven to see it for the nonsense that it is. Though I can no longer, like the swallow, keep myself free of myself by *overlooking my presence*, I can and I do *find myself* to be the space it happens in. Though I can no longer afford, like the young child, to *forget* my feet and what they are treading on, I can and I do *remember* (remember to see) their dissolution. When there is an awareness of nobody walking here in the forest, the walk turns out to be good, easy, untiring, and enjoyable. Without such awareness it's hard going. This is experience, not theorizing. The Void, and its ability to cope with the rough and smooth patches of life, is right here for testing — all day and every day.

This unspeakably miraculous Void from which all creatures live, this incredible Know-how that is everyone's, this central Absence-of-body that regulates and animates all the bodies that proceed from it, is One and the same in all. Intrinsically, it is Perfection itself, in man, child, cat, swallow, worm, cell, particle. But how, in that case, do these seeming malfunctions come about, these twisted ankles and stubbed toes along life's ill-paved road?

It will help if we distinguish clearly the three stages or levels of the behavior we have been looking at:

1. The nonhuman being that lives unquestioningly and without obstructions from its central No-thingness, and thereby "knows" what to do, and how and when to do it. True, it is a dedicated specialist, confining itself to its specific life style. It minds its own business. And to what effect! The young garden spider's *first* wheel-web is an

engineering masterpiece, and he never had a lesson in web-building and what webs are for. The sky where I live is sometimes crowded with birds, not always of the same species, flying this way and that. They have no traffic regulations that I know of, no priorities of left or right, or up or down, yet I have still to witness a near miss, let alone a collision. Birds aren't special cases. Every creature is in its own way equally brilliant, and equally clueless.

2. In his own way, of course, man is still more brilliant. He is the great amateur and unspecialist, Nature's unique generalist. There's hardly an animal skill — on land and sea and air — that he cannot emulate, on the whole clumsily, with many mishaps and abuses and frustrations. He is clumsy because he takes on a body to be clumsy with, and he is frustrated and miserable because that body-idea blocks the No-body that he really is. Man ceases to rely for know-how upon his all-knowing, infinitely resourceful Source, and turns to himself — his tiny, handicapped, and ultimately unreal body-mind — for guidance. The outcome, though hugely impressive, is so disastrous that his very survival is threatened.

3. There is a remedy. It doesn't mean going back to the unconsciousness of the animal, and it doesn't mean giving up the immense gains of that human self-consciousness whereby one takes an outsider's view of oneself. It means going on to that real self-consciousness (or rather, Self-consciousness) whereby one takes the insider's view of oneself. It means coming Home again to the spot one occupies and finding it unoccupied. It means clearly seeing and unreservedly handing over to What and Who one has always been, right here at center. It means recapturing, at the highest level, the natural flair, the easy grace and spontaneity which man alone among creatures has managed to suppress. And it comes to this. The only sensible way to walk through the forest is to see there's nobody doing it.

THE POWER
OF
POSITIVE THINKING

For more than a hundred years the presses have been pouring out a flood of books about the alleged power of positive thinking. They claim to teach the reader "the science of mental magic," or "how to work miracles through will-power or concentration," or "how to realize one's ambitions by means of visualization and self-suggestion," and so forth. While they differ widely — varying from the crudest materialism to a rather facile spirituality — they all draw on the incontrovertible fact that one's health, wealth, and success are largely governed by one's mental attitude. Anyone who is optimistic, resolute, committed, an ardent believer in the goal he or she is aiming at, is very much more likely to get there than someone who is halfhearted and fearful of failure. No doubt about it, positive thinking pays. Nor is it merely that such a frame of mind naturally generates sustained and thorough work, which in turn naturally generates success. More than this, it's as if the mind itself acts directly, you could say magically, on things and people, hiddenly influencing them in the desired direction.

Until one is committed there is hesitation, the chance to draw back, always ineffectiveness. Concerning all acts of initiative there is the elementary truth the ignorance of which kills countless ideas and splendid plans: that the moment one definitely commits oneself Providence moves too. All sorts of things occur to help one that would not otherwise have occurred. A whole stream of events issues from the decision, rais-

ing in one's favor all manner of unforeseen incidents
and meetings and material assistance, which no man
could have dreamed was coming his way. — CHRIS
MURRAY, LEADER OF THE SCOTTISH HIMALAYAN EXPEDITION

Whatever you can do or dream of doing, begin it. Bold-
ness has genius and magic and
power in it. Begin now. — GOETHE

Chris Murray and Goethe are right. The evidence for the effec-
tiveness of this kind of magic is plentiful and convincing. It supports
and is supported by the "idealist" philosophy which claims that the
universe itself is the product of Mind, apart from which it has no substance at all. The world is an elaborate idea. According to this view, so-
called things owe their existence to the fact that they are consistently
and persistently imagined. It follows that an individual's ability to picture his or her future circumstances, projecting them powerfully upon
the shape of things to come, necessarily does much to mould that shape
along the desired lines.

All this is well known. Rather less recognized is the negative side
of this mental magic. Would-be magicians beware! Your spells, woven
out of strong desire and vivid imagination and reinforced by one-
pointed action, are pretty sure to work outwards upon your circumstances; and no less sure to boomerang, to work back powerfully on
you. In the short term you are likely to get more or less what you want
— in skills and goods and recognition — but in the long term you pay
the price, perhaps a very high one. You gain one thing, at the cost — it
may be — of something more subtle and precious. In any case it's
unlikely that your magical successes will find you much happier or
fulfilled than before. As for the ultimate goal of complete and lasting
blessedness, there's no reason for supposing that any amount of mental magic will bring it an inch closer. Rather the reverse.

There are two main alternatives to this sort of mental magic. The
first is to muddle along as usual, thinking and feeling positively or
negatively as the mood takes one and attempting no magic and no
miracles — hoping for the best and fearing the worst, and getting
some of both. Call it the *normal* attitude, in contrast to the *magical*.
Whereas the ordinary man says "My will be done — I hope," and the
magician says "My will be done — I insist," the mystic says "Thy will be

done — I know." His aim is to submit with his whole heart at all times and in all things to what *is*, to God's designs for him as perfectly displayed in his present circumstances, and to leave his future entirely in God's hands. The normal man would like to win, the magician is determined to win, the mystic is content to surrender. His attitude could not be more different from theirs.

Yet here's a very curious thing, a contradiction which has puzzled me for years and is my main reason for writing this chapter — in the hope of clearing up the matter at last. I'm referring to the strange fact that the authors of the saner and sounder of these books, advocating mental magic and positive thinking, aren't content with doing that, but also urge us to place our life in God's hands, to sail with and not against His wind, to swim with and not against His current. I have been startled to find they betray no sense that they are contradicting themselves and proposing an impossibility — not just in theory, but — more importantly — in practice. How on earth can the mood, the attitude which announces "I'm going to get what I want by working a miracle!" co-exist with the mood which says "The one real Miracle is already in progress — the incredible Miracle of His Self-origination, of His Being in Whose perfection I fully share, and Whose arrangements for me must be perfect too?"

For our example of this confusion in thinking (and, inevitably, in practice) let us take one of the earliest and best of these books — Ralph Waldo Trine's *In Tune with the Infinite*. Here is a typical excerpt:

> This is the law of prosperity: When apparent adversity comes, be not cast down by it, but make the best of it, and always look forward for better things, for conditions more prosperous. To hold yourself in this attitude of mind is to set in operation subtle, silent and irresistible forces that sooner or later will actualize in material form that which is today merely an idea. But ideas have occult power, and ideas, when rightly planted and tended, are the seeds that actualize material conditions.
>
> Never give a moment to complaint, but utilize the time that would otherwise be spent in this way in looking forward and actualizing the conditions you desire. Suggest prosperity to yourself. See yourself in a prosperous condition. Affirm it quietly and calmly, but

strongly and confidently. Believe it, believe it absolutely. Expect it, keep it constantly watered with expectation. You thus make yourself a magnet to attract
the things that you desire. Don't be afraid to suggest,
to affirm these things, for by doing so you put forth
an ideal which will begin to clothe itself in material
form. In this way you are utilizing agents among the
most subtle and powerful in the universe.

This is sheer, unadulterated, unashamed magic, poles apart from
the spirituality of the world's saints and sages. Yet elsewhere in the
very same book we read:
Life then ceases to be a plodding, and moves along
day after day much as the tides flow, much as the planets move in their courses, much as the seasons come
and go.
All the frictions, all the uncertainties, all the ills,
the sufferings, the fears, the forebodings, the perplexi-
ties of life come to us because we are out of harmony
with the divine order of things. They will continue to
come as long as we so live. Rowing against the tide is
hard and uncertain. To go with the tide and thus to
take advantage of the working of a great natural force
is safe and easy. To come into the conscious, vital realization of our oneness with the Infinite Life and Power
is to come into the current of this divine sequence.
Coming thus into harmony with the Infinite brings us
in turn into harmony with all about us.

Note which Trine puts first and foremost here — the Infinite —
and which second and subsidiary — the finite. In this excerpt his priorities are those of real spirituality, not of magic. This is no ordinary
and excusable inconsistency: it runs deep. Nor is he alone. In many of
the better therapies and seminars and trainings that are on offer nowadays, as well as in their voluminous literature, the same confusion or
double-talk is all too apparent.
With one breath they urge us to rouse ourselves and harness all
our powers of imagination and desire to work the miracles that will
transform the world, or at least make our lives work the way we want

them to work; and with the next breath they urge us to abandon craving and choose what *is* and recognize in what happens to us our deepest intention.

If you feel that I'm finding a contradiction in strategy where there is only a tactical variation, or that I'm exaggerating the difficulty of reconciling these two attitudes, please consider what the world's spiritual leaders have to say on the subject of getting what you want. Somebody asked Ramana Maharshi how he could develop willpower. Maharshi replied: "Your idea of willpower is success assured. (Real) willpower is the strength of mind which meets success or failure with equanimity ... Why should one's efforts be attended by success? Success develops arrogance and one's spiritual progress is thus arrested. Failure, on the other hand is beneficial, inasmuch as it opens one's eyes to one's limitations and prepares one to surrender oneself. Self-surrender is synonymous with happiness." And Rumi, the greatest of the Sufi masters, went so far as to declare: "Unsuccess is the guide to Paradise." How remote this is from the philosophy that brands the very thought of failure as sick and life-denying and accompanied by every sort of wretchedness! All the great spiritual traditions insist that Liberation (alias Salvation, Enlightenment, Self-realization, Awakening) is at least as consistent with what the world calls abject failure as with success. A vivid illustration of this sobering fact is the following story — parable, rather — of Meister Eckhart's:

> God said to him: "Go to the church and there you will find a man who will show you the way to blessedness." There he found a poor man whose feet were torn and covered with dust and dirt, and all his clothes were hardly worth three farthings. And he greeted that poor man, saying:
> "God give you a good day."
> "I have never had a bad day," he answered.
> "God give you good luck."
> "I have never had ill luck."
> "May you be happy. But why do you answer me thus?"
> "I have never been unhappy."
> "Pray explain this to me, for I cannot understand it."
> "Willingly," the poor man answered, "You wished me a good day, I have never had a bad day, for if I am hungry I praise God; if it freezes, hails, snows, rains, if the

weather is fair or foul still I praise God. Am I wretched
and despised? I praise God. And so I have never had
an evil day. You wished that God would send me luck.
But I have never had bad luck, for I know how to live
with God and I know that what He does is best. And
what God gives me or ordains for me, be it good or ill,
I take it cheerfully from God as the best that can be,
and so I never have ill luck. You wished that God would
make me happy. I was never unhappy, for my only desire is to live in God's will. And I have so entirely yielded
my will to God's that *what God wills I will*."

Is this positive thinking or negative thinking? Beyond question
this is *absolutely* positive thinking. Compared with Eckhart's poor man,
who indeed had reason to call himself a king, the most aggressively
optimistic and effervescent and positive of mental magicians is hesi-
tant and on his guard and at least partially negative. For his magic to
work at all it has to work against resistance, against circumstances that
he finds undesirable and in need of changing. Thus his positivity is
necessarily partial and conditioned by the negativity it requires and
combats. Not so the positive thinking of Eckhart's poor man, which is
unconditional and unlimited. As Ramana Maharshi points out, "Identity with Brahman places the man in harmony with *everything*, and there
is nothing apart from the Self."

So our criticism of the practitioners of mental magic — of the
positive thinking which needs and even creates negative resistance to
pit itself against — is that, though they have the right idea, they don't
carry it nearly far enough. They are insufficiently positive, indeed insufficiently expert at magic. The only way to unleash irresistible magic,
and to think and feel without any negativity, is consciously to station
oneself where one has always been anyway, namely at the source of it
all, at the unthinkable Origin which is the only real Magician and the
only real Power and the only real Affirmation free from any trace of
denial. Rejoin that sole and only positive Source, and see what your
life is like.

Which raises the big question: "If my thinking and feeling were to
approach absolute positivity and I said a hearty "Yes!" to everything,
would I bother to plan or to achieve anything at all? Would I go to the
trouble of getting up in the morning, and having a shower and dress-

ing and making myself breakfast — not to mention going out and earning a living? Here, surely, is a recipe for paralysis."

Actually the problem exists only in theory. When it comes to practice you will find that your behavior, looked at from outside, is normal enough. As for the inside, it's not that you see something wrong, some negativity, in God's otherwise perfect arrangements, and strenuously try to make good that deficiency by positive thinking and action. No: rather it is that, as Aware Space for the world, you are forever the same and free of ideas or intention or drive or action, while the world that fills this Space is *all* ideas and intention and drive and action, ever on the move, ever upsetting and correcting the old by means of the new. And this busy scene includes your hands and what they do, and your feet and where they go, and the sounds that issue from here. In other words, Who you really, really are doesn't initiate action (the No-thing here does nothing) but finds it going on anyhow. These hands and this typewriter are at this moment producing these words, and there's no experience of somebody here intent on stringing the words together. Right here, nothing is initiated, no separate and special events are being contrived and set in motion. They are witnessed. The flow of these words is no more (and no less) the product of intention than the flow of the river and of the clouds in the sky.

Returning, then, to our question: when you consciously become Who you are anyway (and accordingly your attitude is wholly accepting and positive) *will you as a human being turn out to be less (or more) positive and creative and energetic as you start living from the truth that intrinsically you aren't a human being at all?*

The answer is: *see Who you are at center, and then see what you get up to out there. Be prepared to tap undreamed-of energies.* The history of the true Seers demonstrates that they were much more effective than the average person. Clearly some of them changed the course of history. What would this species of ours be like without its saints and sages and their immense efforts on its behalf?

They were the great ones. You, dear reader, are no different essentially. You also begin thinking and feeling and acting positively in the absolute sense directly you wake to your true Nature. And, as Ramana Maharshi tirelessly pointed out, waking to that Nature is the simplest and most natural thing you could ever do. You have only to stop pretending.

In conclusion, there's no way up from the very partial positive thinking, which Trine and Company Limited advocate, to the Absolute Positivity that you already are. The traffic is all in the other direction, down from its products to its Ground in the depth of you. So it all comes to a question of getting your priorities right, of putting first things first. "Seek ye first the Kingdom of God and His justice, and all these things shall be added." No accumulation or manipulation of these things will get you an inch nearer the Kingdom — the Kingdom you never left. "Find the Self," says Maharshi, "and all problems are solved." Ignore the Self, and no amount of positive thinking or mental magic will get you out of trouble.

TRANSUBSTANTIATION

No religious dogma that has meant great things to great numbers
of people over the centuries is likely to be altogether false or
absurd. Nor is it likely to be altogether true and workable for us now in
its traditional form. The chances are that, as a vehicle of truth, it is
breaking down — or at least slowing down — and that it needs not so
much minor repairs on the one hand, nor scrapping on the other, as a
thorough overhaul. So the question to ask about such a dogma isn't "Is
it true?" but rather "In what sense and at what level is it true and
meaningful for us at this time?" The resulting answer could well prove
very valuable indeed. Not a specious and popular new look superimposed on the same old creaking machinery, but a profound penetration to its original and hidden design. It may then be possible to see in
that design more than the designers were fully conscious of, so that it
and they are valued more highly than ever. And, for bonus, a further
result could be the settlement of disputes that have torn the religious
establishment apart for centuries.

Nor can we dodge such a radical overhauling on the plea that
"spiritual" truth, unlike "scientific" and "everyday" truth, is sacrosanct.
There is only one sort of truth — the sort that sets men free. A doctrine
ceases to make sense in religion when in every other field it is seen to
be nonsense. It isn't true on Sunday if it's false the rest of the week.
The genuinely spiritual contradicts common sense (which of course it
very often does) because it sees through socially conditioned nonsense
to what really does make sense. For true spirituality is transparently

honest, simple (and therefore difficult), accurate, and sharper than a razor.

These are bald assertions, but they can be illustrated. Take, for instance, the ancient and revered dogma of transubstantiation in the Eucharist, according to which the whole substance of the bread and the wine is changed into Christ's flesh and blood, only the appearance of bread and wine remaining.

Well, what was the body of Jesus Christ really like, not as seen by others but *in his own firsthand experience?* Let us consult him on this matter and take him at his word, since no one else is in a position to speak for him. What he tells us all to do he surely did himself: becoming as a little child he saw, within himself, not a convoluted mass of anatomical plumbing but the Kingdom of Heaven. His Eye being single, his whole body was also full of Light, having no place dark. Leaving aside theological speculation, let us suppose he meant just what he said, and that he spoke not metaphorically but literally, in terms that would be understood by little children. In that case, he saw his body as actually replaced by the Light that lights everyone that comes into the world. This Light was what he really was, his interior secret, the true inside story that read so differently from the outside story of his appearance to others. Which body, then, does he offer to the communicant in the Mass — the seeming one or the real one, the outer human one (which would make the communicant a cannibal) or the inner divine one? Obviously the latter. And the truly enlightened communicant accepts it as such, as the opaque matter of earth transubstantiated into the clear Light of Heaven.

Nor can our enlightened communicant stop at that immensely important realization. Taking the words of his Lord seriously, he sees that he, too, is all Light within. Childlike, he notices, with thankful astonishment, that he too is furnished with a single Eye which takes in the Kingdom's boundless and immaculate brilliance. Indeed it is his own interior Light which alone enables him to receive from the officiating priest the true body of the Lord, so that the light entering the Light is not darkened and communion becomes union.

What can all this mean to the honest and open-minded skeptic of today? It can make perfect sense — provided he is really open to the evidence. Speaking for myself, I find that the miracle of transubstantiation is reenacted at every meal. Of course the bread there on my dining table has the ordinary appearance of bread, crust and crumb, and the wine glows red, as wine should — when viewed from this dining chair. But when I put forth a hand to bring them to me, and they traverse the distance of a foot or so that separates us, they are mysteriously and marvelously transformed. I watch them grow, become blurred, lose form and texture and color, and then vanish altogether, not into a mouth and throat but into this immense and empty Maw. Undone and "spiritualized" by stages on their way to me, they are voided into this Void, visibly absorbed into the Clarity which is my true Nature. If they are eaten and drunk, then this is a very different sort of eating and drinking from the strange goings-on over there in the other dining chairs, where absolutely insipid foreign substances are being poked into toothed slits in people's faces. Here, by contrast, edible and potable things are becoming unthinged and merging with the No-thing that I am. All eating and drinking by the First Person as such (emphatically not by the third-person as such) is a veritable Holy Communion whenever it is realized to be just that.

Thus the believing communicant isn't mistaken. The miracle of the Eucharist is neither a pious fraud nor a beautiful but dying myth. The innermost story of the Lord at the Last Supper with his disciples in Jerusalem, of the present bread and wine on the altar, of the celebrant and of the communicant himself, is one and the same story. However different their date and circumstances, at heart they are one and the same. Here are facts that can be verified by anyone interested.

There is a place where Catholics with their transubstantiation, Lutherans with their consubstantiation, other Churches with their own variations on the theme, and even Humanists and Positivists with their science-inspired rejection of all religious dogmas, can come together without compromising their basic convictions, but rather clarifying and deepening them. That place is this place, now, right where you are at this moment at no distance from yourself. Transubstantiation, the miraculous switchover from appearance to Reality, from accident to Essence, from so many shades of darkness to the One Light, can never be observed from a distance, remembered, or anticipated. It doesn't happen elsewhere or elsewhen. Out there, bodies put up a show, they keep up appearances, veil upon veil, but the veils cover one indivisible and Self-luminous Substance, all of it on show right now and right here, awaiting instant inspection. This is that one Sight which it is imperative to see, and the one which, happily, can never be mis-seen. More happily still, it is quite obvious and natural and ordinary, as soon as it

AN OPEN-EYED
MAN FALLING
INTO A WELL

A monk asked Zen master Haryo, "What is the way?"
Haryo answered, "An open-eyed man falling into a well."

W ill you please picture this world of delusion-based suffering (all
stemming from the fiction "I am this separate human") as a flat
landscape, wearing an overall sameness? Except, that is, for a single
outstanding landmark. Dominating the countryside is a Castle that
combines the features and functions of a sacred temple, a strong fortress, and a healing center. There it stands for all to see — for all who
want to see — this shrine whose motto, carved above the doorway, is "I
AM." It extends to everyone the prospect of a safe refuge from danger,
certain therapy for every ill, and all the comfort of the holiest.

And what happens?

The nearly universal pretence is that this magnificent Castle doesn't
exist at all, or else is an apparition or mirage. The great majority of the
population turn a blind eye to it, don't spare it a second thought. Some,
however, do take notice and draw near and explore the structure's walls
and battlements and turrets from outside, tentatively. A few muster the
courage to peep inside from time to time. But for almost all that's
quite enough, thank you very much. A powerful instinct warns them
off. They sense an unknown danger, as terrifying as the worst of those
that lie in wait for them outside. Nor, as we shall presently see, are they
entirely wrong.

Driven to desperation by his plight in the world, or fascinated by the mystery and the splendor of the Castle, or more likely for no conscious reason at all, the odd adventurer sets foot inside.

The disillusion is severe and immediate. Within, the splendid fortress of "I AM" is roofless and quite empty, a mere shell, a showy facade.

Worse is to come, much worse. Nervously picking his way to the dim interior, his foot finds no floor. He is pitched into a chasm that seemingly is bottomless. And not only does his fall go on and on, but it plunges him into depths where he's progressively stripped of every vestige of humanness, of thought and feeling and mind in general, of life, of existence, even of consciousness. The promised stronghold and life-refuge of "I AM" turns out to be a mere bait for the fatal trap of "I AM NOT."

So much for our parable. Let us turn now to what some exceptionally open-eyed fallers into the well have to say about their experience, and discover how they have sought to raise to consciousness this depth on depth of unconsciousness and to extol its priority and power.

The author of the *Tao Te Ching* exhausts himself in his search for apt names for this strictly nameless abyss. It is nonbeing, darker than any mystery, empty, lower than low, elusive, blank, incomprehensible, shadowy, dim, dull, useless, thin, flavorless, even depressing. On the other hand, and just because it is so all of these things, it depends on nothing and is inexhaustible, the well that never runs dry. And so — wonder of wonders! — the ultimate Negative is revealed as the ultimate Positive.

What is it like in practice to be so engulfed in unconsciousness, so poverty-stricken, so unable to arrive at any bottoming-out of our lack and lucklessness, so robbed of any basis for our life? D.T. Suzuki has the answer. "How rich," he exclaims, "is the inward life of the man of Zen, because it is in direct communication with the great unconscious ... This unknown, once recognized, enters into ordinary consciousness and puts into good order all the complexities there which have been tormenting us to greater or lesser degrees... As soon as it is recognized that our consciousness comes out of something which, though not known in the way relative things are known, is intimately related to us, we are relieved of every form of tension and are thoroughly at rest and at peace with ourselves and with the world generally." Such are the heartening words that float up from one who is falling forever from the known I AM into the unknowable I AM NOT.

Here Suzuki is echoing the early Zen master Hui-neng and his essential doctrine of no-mind, according to which our self-nature realizes itself as emptiness and nowhereness. This lively awareness of the depths of the great unconscious — this leaning back on no support — is the fundamental requirement in the life of Zen. And Hubert Benoit is echoing both Hui-neng and Suzuki when he declares: "You are unhappy because you are established in consciousness instead of in the unconscious."

Which gives rise to the conundrum: how can the unconscious rise to become conscious without ceasing to be itself, without leaving behind what distinguishes it from consciousness? As if darkness, tired of obscurity and craving attention, were to insist on coming to light.

Zen has its own solution to the puzzle, one that's all the more convincing in practice because it defies the analytical intellect. In an inspired image, Hui-hai (one of Hui-neng's successors) declares: "Prajna — that perfection of wisdom which is our true nature — is unconscious, but facing the yellow flowers it functions." Much later, the Japanese Soto master Dogen has this famous passage: "To pursue Buddhism is to pursue the self, to pursue the self is to lose the self, to lose the self is to be enlightened by all other beings." Not, please note, to enlighten them, but the reverse. And by what other means, we may well ask, could the unconscious be enlightened about itself, but by seeing what it comes up with? — what it comes up from is inscrutable darkness, in which there's nothing to be enlightened about. Later still, Eugen Herrigel, drawing on the same tradition and his own experience, had this to say: "All things, seen from their origin, are equal, have an absolute value. Their origin and ground can be perceived only through them. You see, with absolute certainty, that things *are* by virtue of what they *are not*. To the degree that their formless origin is inaccessible and inconceivable, things in their concrete form become more accessible. Bathed in the light of their origin, they themselves are illuminated." All of which is summed up in the great saying of Zen: *Nirvana* is *Samsara*. Without *Samsara* there is no *Nirvana*. To adopt and adapt Hui-hai's terms, in the yellow flowers at it's mouth, the bottomless well comes into its own.

Let me put the whole matter rather differently. In this and other chapters of this book it has been necessary to insist on the absolute contrast between the nest of one's appearances and the central mystery they arise from. The time has come to transcend this most fundamental of distinctions. Sloughing off the many layers of what I look like to others, I concentrate on the one here that sheds them, only to find a vacuum. If I have or am a central reality at all, it is those regional appearances — all of them at all ranges, as revealed to all observers. In the end I am all integument, skin laid on skin, with nothing at their core. I wonder whether Oscar Wilde ever guessed the profundity of his joke: "Reality is keeping up appearances?"

It may come as a mild shock to some of you that a number of the great Christian mystics, not content with announcing the intrinsic nothingness of all created beings, extend the same treatment to their Creator. The God they describe is an absentee, an absconder, in himself the most Nothing of all nothings. Losing track of himself altogether, he finds himself in the other, in his beloved Son, and through him in all his many sons and daughters. Here is the undiscriminating love that vanishes without trace in favor of the loved one. Such is the divine nature, in whose image we are all built. Thus Meister Eckhart, "The end is the mystery of the darkness of the eternal Godhead, and it is unknown and never will be known. God dwells therein unknown to himself ... Seek him in such a way that you will never find him ... He is a not-God, a not-mind, neither a person nor an image. Sink eternally from something to nothing in him." Eckhart's disciple Tauler speaks of "the fathomless abyss, bottomless and floating in itself, which is much more God's dwelling than heaven or man is." And that remarkable woman, the Blessed Angela of Foligno, has this to say: "I put all my hope in a secret good, which I apprehend in a great darkness. All creatures filled with God, the divine power and will — all is inferior to this most hidden good. The other things bring delight, but this vision of God in darkness brings no smile to the lips, no devotion or fervor to the soul ... Yet all the countless and unspeakable words and favors of God to me are so inferior to this vision of God in darkness that I put no trust in them at all." And, with unmatched conviction and eloquence, the Blessed Jan van Ruysbroeck finds the darkness and the light coming together in the fathomless. If we could know the incomprehensible light it would have mode and measure, and then it could never satisfy us. Only because it is ineffable and abysmal is this "wild darkness of the Godhead" our sure refuge.

And now, just to show that the Sufi masters, too, are with us, here is Rumi: "A Somewhat that is not to be found — that is my goal."

Finally, I would like to add my own testimony. I certainly don't find myself on the brink of a bottomless abyss, trying to make up my mind whether to let go and take that dreadful plunge. I'm already clear of the brink and free-falling, and have never been otherwise. To see this, all I have to do is look for myself, and fail to find myself, and find instead the treasure that has no name in the well at the world's end.

JUST
LIKE THE
IVY

He who binds to himself a joy
Doth the winged life destroy;
But he who kisses the joy as it flies
Lives in eternity's sunrise
— WILLIAM BLAKE

The title of this chapter is taken from a popular song of the early 1900s: *Just like the Ivy, I'll Cling to You*. It neatly sums up the story of my life — well, let's say most of it. Ivy isn't too fussy about what it clings to. Old walls and gutters and roofs will do if trees aren't around. But cling it must, to something. Just like the ivy, I have found myself clinging to a succession of contrasting supports, for very life. Here I want to give some account of them, from infancy onwards.

GRASPING THE PHYSICAL
As a baby I attached myself, hungrily, to my mother's breast. I demanded and got those encouraging warmths and sounds and smells, those cuddling arms, those caressing hands and lips without which I could barely survive, let alone flourish. Then came, in place of the withheld breast, my thumb, then my rattle, my teddy, my other toys. And later, my collections of all sorts from marbles and seashells and fossils to coins and cigarette cards and postage stamps. What an obsessional collector I was, and none too particular about what the collection consisted of! This juvenile curator hugged to himself, in a sense

he became his treasure exhibits. He lived in and for, and through them.

And all the time I was putting together a very different sort of exhibit — a physique to attach these possessions to. At first, the rattle and the hand that held it weren't sharply distinguished. They were, so to say, continuous. The progressive discovery and outlining of that uniquely sensitive region of my universe which I learned to call my body was my progressive identification with it, over against the rest of things. This became little me, set in an enormous not-me. And the more I clung to the former the less I fitted into the latter.

All the same, throughout those wonderful years up to eight or so, my embodiment or incarnation remained incomplete. This body-thing that accompanied me everywhere was increasingly experienced as mine, but I wasn't in it. Except when miserable or faulted, I remained a place for things to happen in, rather than one of those things. Accordingly my world was still fascinating and marvelous. The meanest smudge of color or fallen leaf or dewdrop held magic — until, claiming it for myself, I spoiled it. The gorgeous butterfly that in my fist was reduced to a mess might have warned me that the surest way to lose anything is to clutch at it.

The years from around eight completed the process. Painfully I pulled myself together. Under severe pressure from all around me, reinforced by an inner need, I collected and assembled and set up, on top of that clearly visible torso, a visualized finial or protuberance consisting of a head with unique features, a thousand facial expressions, an entire persona. Till now I had left all that stuff where it belonged — out there in mirrors and cameras, and for people to make what they liked of. But now, mistaking that regional appearance for my central reality, I latched on to it, to have and to hold tight for the rest of my life. And so I became, for myself here, what I looked like over there. Which makes no sense at all.

For me this absurd but normal maneuver worked very badly. Trading my immense and real space for that tiny and imaginary face — imaginary here — was an agonizing transaction. The latter took all the blame. I became convinced that my face, my nose in particular, was hideous, a laughing stock. With ups and downs, my exaggerated and sometimes pathological bashfulness lasted well into my twenties, and was apt to crop up — to my great distress at the worst possible moments — as late as my early thirties. I remained shame-faced. I loathed the thing. But it was a love-hate relationship. The worse time it gave me, the more I hung onto it.

GRASPING THE MENTAL

Along with this painful acquisition of a separate and central body-thing went the painful acquisition of a separate and central mind-thing.

As a young child I had, strictly speaking, no mind of my own, no personal and private psyche, no inner world of thoughts and feelings detached from their proper objects in the world. At that comparatively happy stage it wasn't a case of "I'm furious with you" but of "You are horrible." Or of "I love those primroses" but of "They are lovely." It wasn't that I was frightened of goblins, but that the cellar of our house was infested with the frightful creatures. Not I but places were sad, or thoughtful, or jumpy, or terrifying. In fact my world was marvelously rich with interlocking meanings and emotions in the same way, as it was marvelously rich with primary and secondary colors and sounds and tastes and smells. All too briefly, my mind and my world were one and the same. And it was because I didn't clasp it to myself here that it was so brilliant, so magical.

And then I began collecting a mind of my own, to inhabit and bug the body that I was simultaneously collecting here. Increasingly, my feelings and thoughts about my world were no longer simply about it, but about me, subjective impressions, states of mind. Thus, piece by piece, I built up here my private and ever more complex inner world, at the expense of that outer world, the objective universe. In the end I was full to bursting and my world was a meaningless machine. Both were sick.

Just as that originally acceptable face in the mirror became increasingly unacceptable when I took it in and hugged it to myself here, so also did those originally acceptable thoughts and feelings about the world become increasingly unacceptable when they were about me the subject here, rather than about their objects over there. They failed to stand up to the inward journey, got spoiled on the way in. By claiming and clinging to this elaborate and make-believe abstraction called my mind, instead of letting it remain at large, I obstructed its workings and darkened it all with much anxiety and frequent anguish. The trouble with my mind was that I spoiled it by claiming it.

GRASPING THE SPIRITUAL

Strange to relate, clinging for support to the body and then the mind wasn't enough. I went on to clutch at a third entity, by some called the Spirit, by others the impersonal Self or Consciousness, and by me called the feeling that here I Am. I don't mean the feeling of being this particular person, but of simply being here. In fact this sense was, however vaguely, here from the start. And all my subsequent clinging stemmed from the tacit assumption that there is one here who clings.

But I find a striking difference between my clinging to body and mind on the one hand and to spirit on the other. The first two plainly grew more painful and cramping and sick and in the end ridiculous, whereas the third had a wonderful way of concealing its hurt and its harm. The truth is that, when fully developed, this sense of HERE I AM can and does set itself up as liberation, the true letting go. In fact, it's nothing of the sort. The medieval author of *The Cloud of Unknowing* saw it for what it is. "All men have matter for sorrow, but most specially he feeleth matter for sorrow that knoweth and feeleth that he is. All other sorrows in comparison with this be but as it were game to earnest."

In my own case this ultimate distress remained, for far too long, repressed, unconscious. To be Myself here, all present and correct, was to be onto a good thing. Little did I know!

So much for the first part of my story, the clinging half. I come now to the second part, the letting-go half.

LETTING THE PHYSICAL GO

It all began when, quite casually, I happened to take a look at the spot I occupy, and found it unoccupied. At once I saw how crazy I had been to superimpose what I look like upon what I am, and then to lock onto that fictional superimposition for dear life. How refreshing it was, how good even for the body, to relax one's stranglehold on it and let it go to where it belongs! Nor was this a partial seeing-off of the incubus from here to there. Of this absence there are no degrees.

Need I add that this seeing-off was at first momentary, and that it took many years and much practice before it became habitual? By practice I mean renewal of the original experience and not — repeat *not* — adding anything to it. And by habitual I mean remaining in contact with one's central clarity and not — repeat *not* — clinging to it. Not demanding that it should remain in the forefront of one's attention in all the changing circumstances of life. Much of the time it has to be —

it needs to be — in the background, and, like one's friends, neither lost nor inescapable and always on the agenda, on hold but not hung onto. The alternative is a crippling obsession. "In darkness are they who only look outwards, but in thicker darkness are they who only look within." The seer who said that said a true thing. I'm reminded, too, of Wodehouse on the subject of holidays: their healing charm is fresh air and fresh faces and fresh scenery — and the absence of loved ones!

LETTING THE MENTAL GO

And so once more I became what, though less consciously, I had been as a young child — the huge arena for the show, for every kind of thing to happen in. But, oh dear! One of those things happened to be my firmly rooted conviction that — body or no body — I certainly am a mind. That right here at the center is a hold-all stuffed full of *my* sensations and feelings and thoughts and memories and hopes and fears and I don't know what else. And certainly I found that dispersing the mental contents of my head wasn't half so easy as dispersing their physical container. It takes a long while to unpack and see off all that mental clobber, and rest in the discovery that right here is no trace of it. Nor, in my experience, is it seen off once and for all. This bugbear, or specter, I call my mind, has a nasty habit of coming back again and again relentlessly, and my job is to cultivate the habit of seeing it off every time. Or, let's say, ceasing to cling to the thing and letting it go to where it belongs. This is the ever-renewed discovery that I have no *inner* world, no thoughts and feelings of my very own. Pain and pleasure are way off center. I find no joy here: I rejoice in those dear ones over there, in those flowers alight with color, those misty hills, those soaring mountain peaks. To find out what I'm thinking I listen to you and him and her. To discover my political views I turn on the television and read the papers — left, right, and center. History makes up my mind for me on social and economic issues. I am truly broad-minded to the degree that my mind, let go of, alights on and merges with and irradiates the whole scene. There it comes into its own. To be opinionated, narrow-minded, under pressure, depressed, repressed — all such diseases of the mind arise from its displacement and resulting compression. Given back to the world, returned to where it came from, it expands and recovers. At large again, it is infinitely large and generous.

LETTING THE SPIRITUAL GO

Having released my stranglehold on body and mind and packed them off to their proper place, had I then vanished without trace? Quite the contrary. Though I'm no longer this or that or the other, I still AM. It would seem that, hanging onto those comparatively brief and trivial identities, I had underrated myself absolutely. "I am Douglas Harding" cannot be compared with "I AM" for peace and comfort, for safety and security, for magnificence, yes, even for naturalness. I AM is such a noble name, and it feels right. And, for God's sake, it *is* all right! But HERE it's all wrong.

I had been saying to myself — unconsciously, but all the more insistently because unconsciously — "I can safely lose all trace of body, of mind, even of Spirit, so long as there remains here that bare sense of undifferentiated Being or Awareness without which nothing remains but oblivion, eternal death and annihilation, the abyss of the inane, and all is lost forever and forever. I simply dare not let go of this last support, this most prestigious and holy and permanent and reliable of props."

For too long this was my refuge, my bunker. Then something unknown happened to blow up that bunker, to knock away that superprop. And, amazingly, all was well, very well indeed, exceedingly well. The terror, the fear of total extinction, had been baseless.

At this point it's necessary to go back for a bit.

In a sense I have all my life been very fortunate, inasmuch as my basic problems, having been exceptionally severe and exaggerated, called for and got exceptionally radical solutions. Or, at any rate, solutions that overwhelmed and captivated me. A quite exceptionally faced-up youngster, I needed to become exceptionally conscious of the remedy. My acquired face had been so excruciatingly ill-fitting that my Original Face was bound to come as a profound relief. Again, burdened here with a very heavy load of introspective and anxious mind-stuff, I had powerful motives for relocating it. And finally, my passion for the Real and True, for the Source, for "the Perfection of Wisdom, the lovely, the holy," for the mystery and majesty and splendor of God — this has been the driving force of the greater part of my life. And my hope is that its "cure," its ejection from here, has been equally thoroughgoing. Oh the relief! How necessary this spring-cleaning! If this is a contradiction, it's the sort that made reverent and dedicated Buddhists "wash their mouths after talking of the Buddha," and plan to kill him if he came too near: he's for polishing off if he can't be seen off. And it's the sort that made the equally reverent and dedicated Eckhart dismiss God or Spirit from the center, in favor of the Not-God and Not-Spirit, the Desert which no foot has ever trod. In short, just as body and mind are truly realized and invigorated by seeing them off from here to there, so also is Spirit. All the varieties of religious and mystical experience one ever enjoyed, evicted from the central position they never in fact occupied, come into their own as they are restored to the world, to the manifested universe which is replete at last with all those qualities, physical and mental *and spiritual,* which are its own. Here can be found none of all that, but only the clean cool air of ... No, it's better not to try to stick a label on this surfaceless Abyss.

And so, along with Kierkegaard, I find that my life has been lived forwards and understood backwards. With the benefit of hindsight, I am hugely grateful to have been not only just like the ivy, but like that sort of ivy which is so tenacious that it pulls down every support.

AN ANTI-CLINGING DEVICE

You may feel that in the foregoing I have been putting down the body and the mind, and more particularly the Spirit or I AMness, in favor of Nothingness or I am not. And that this is nihilism at its most negative and the ultimate counsel of despair. And moreover that it contradicts some of the rest of what I say in this book, and specially my insistence on our need to graduate from "I am this and that" to "I AM."

I hasten to assure you that, on the contrary, my aim here is not to put down but in a very true sense put up Spirit and mind and body, so that all three are more highly valued and rise to their proper places in the scheme of things.

Here we have a communication problem. To talk or write about a succession of valuables is to present them one after the other in linear fashion, as if they were separable and not interdependent, or perhaps as if they were a series of incompatibles from which we have to choose one or another. This surreptitious substitution of *or* for *and* is one of the most serious handicaps of the spoken and written word.

The remedy I prescribe is to present these seeming incompatibles together and not separately, in global instead of linear fashion, so that their connections are indicated at a glance and they are seen to support one another instead of competing for our assent. In short, what's needed is a map of the whole country. Such as the one below:

Among the messages this map has for me are these:

Yes, Spirit by itself, the Awareness and the I AM and the Being that *has to be*, that automatically is its sole self from all eternity, is wonderful. But infinitely more wonderful is the Spirit and the Being that doesn't *have* to be, the Awareness that with no help and for no reason continually arises from Unawareness, from Nothing whatsoever — thereby making that Nothing extremely precious as well as indispensable. By virtue of this Nothing it's not *what* Spirit is but *that* it is, which is so breathtakingly adorable. Much the same applies to the arising of our entire Body-Mind (which is none other than the universe) with no help and for no reason, from bare Spirit. What a universe it is, what incredible richness and variety gush tirelessly from this unutterably simple I AM which I am!

In short, I find this map to be a valuable antidote against clinging. It reminds me of the fact that to lock onto any of its parts, in isolation from the living and strictly indivisible Whole, is to undervalue and to spoil both part and Whole, if not to kill them outright.

I hope you, too, will find it useful.

TALES

OF

TENDERNESS

Among all the occasions of tenderness in my life four or five stand out. In this chapter I shall briefly tell them, and go on to make some deductions about the nature of tenderness and how it may possibly be cultivated, or at least be encouraged.

My first story appears so trivial as to be hardly worth telling. It is an early but vivid memory. I had fallen and hurt my knee, and my father "made it better," as he put it, by pressing a penny on the spot. I can't imagine why this quite typical act of his seemed to me so perfect and so beautiful, or why I love him more for this than for any of the countless and immensely more important things he had ever done for me.

Looking back, I suspect that all the occasions of real tenderness in my life have been like this — absurd, out of all proportion, and quite unpredictable. This surely is part of their special quality. They are true mystical insights, sudden influxes or effluxes of divine grace, unaccountable, taking one wholly by surprise.

The second example dates from when I was about eleven. I was reading Dickens' *A Tale of Two Cities*. It is the old story of two men in love with the same girl, one of them thoroughly deserving and an eminently suitable match (and desperately dull) and the other a drunken, no-good character called Sidney, who doesn't stand a chance. Unfortunately it is the worthy suitor who lies in prison awaiting the guillotine, while Sidney the failure is at large in the city of Paris — Paris in the throes of revolution. He paces the deserted streets all night working up his courage to do the noble thing and bribe his way into the jail and substitute himself for his condemned rival (whom he closely resembles) and suffer death in his place. He decides, after a painful struggle with himself, to die for his "enemy," and goes on to carry out his plan.

Victorian sentimentality at its corniest, no doubt. But not for me. I remember, immediately after reading this tale, standing in our local railway station in an ecstasy I can't begin to describe, except to say that the whole scene, the very bricks and the paving of the platform and the rails and sleepers were a glory. I stood in heaven, a heaven in which terrible sadness gave way to overwhelming joy. My weeping was over. A warm splendor suffused the world, breath-taking, melting, healing. Was it that, in spite of everything, self-giving love and tenderness are what the universe is really about? Not that I formulated my feeling in that way or any way, or sought an explanation of the secret that was revealed to me standing in that little railway station so long ago. And not that the feeling stayed with me. It lasted, as I recall, only a few hours, and too soon heaven sank and dimmed into earth again. But I knew what tenderness was. The ecstasy went, the revelation has remained to this day.

My third tale dates from some twenty years later. Again, the experience was out of all proportion, ridiculously exaggerated when viewed objectively. A busy street — in what town I can't remember — an old woman, a boy. I saw the boy go up to the old woman, take her hand, and lead her across the street to safety. That's all. I wept. Such a very ordinary little act of kindness, so unlike the spectacular self-sacrifice of Dickens' hero, yet equally cosmic in its significance for me. It seemed to me then, and seems still, a true insight into the heart of things, a revelation which — in a way I can't account for — makes everything all right. The universe that comes up with this sort of thing is this sort of universe.

My fourth tale is, alas, a very different story. I am now middle-aged. I suppose, over the years, I had cultivated a view of myself as a compassionate, tenderhearted, unselfish, caring person, and had tried — with very little success — to live up to this exacting self-image. So that when a young man in great need came to me for help, why of course I helped him. He was homeless, confused, uninteresting but not at all unpleasant — and I took him in (and took myself in) with a suitable show of tenderness. He turned out to be lazy, terribly untidy, happy to be waited on. More importantly, he took my kindness very much for granted, as if I should be grateful for the opportunity to practice unselfishness. Predictably my annoyance — or was it fury? — mounted daily, growing harder and harder to conceal. Well, at last he took off. And as soon as he had safely distanced himself and his nasty habits, why I felt very, very tenderhearted towards him again. Talk of inconsistency, of double standards!

I regret to say that this sorry tale has repeated itself, with many variations, far too often in what I like to think of as my maturer years. All my attempts to cultivate tenderness, to work up the loving feeling, deliberately to express it in acts of kindness and compassion, have ended similarly in failure — at least from my point of view. Possibly the beneficiaries — or victims — of my good deeds did in fact reap some benefits, but at best I was doing the right thing for the wrong reason. If the heart has its reasons they are unknown to the head. I can't speak for you, but I'm sure that my own tenderness is either spontaneous or it is a pose, a pretence, even a fraud, and its deliberate cultivation is as absurd as it is self-defeating.

What, then, can I do about my often deplorable lack of this precious faculty? Nothing at all? Do I have to accept, with resignation if not complacency, this carapace of toughness that is always threatening to enclose me? Tenderness on principle, tenderness worked up in furtherance of my self-image, rings false, if indeed it can momentarily be achieved at all. But surely the genuine article, leading to its practical expression in truly loving behavior, can at least be encouraged? Even if there's no way of deliberately sloughing the hard skin that threatens to separate me from my environment, can't I at least reduce the growth rate of life's callosities? Is there no solvent, no antidote for creeping petrifaction of the heart?

There is. Tenderness is like happiness and most of the other good things in life, a by-product of something else and not for directly aiming at. It really is available, though not on its own level or on its own terms. Actually it is more than *available*. It is *natural*. It is how I am, if only I don't get in its way and obstruct the spontaneous and unpredictable working of my own essentially tender heart.

For what, after all, is tenderness, in the physical or basic sense? A tough joint of beef is one that resists penetration and calls for a saw rather than a knife. A tender joint, on the other hand, is one that offers little resistance to invasion and cuts almost like butter. Substances can be sorted out in order of hardness, from thin air to a diamond. Now where do I fall in the table of softness-hardness? Somewhere in the middle, is the common sense answer, harder than a jellyfish and softer than a tortoise. The true answer is very different indeed. It's not concerned with what sort of stuff I'm made of in others' experience but in my own experience of myself right here. What is the inside story of this halfway tough character? When I examine the spot I occupy — a place to which no outsider has access — what do I find? Does this most neglected of all places, the hub of my ambient universe, offer any resistance to knives and saws, to people, to Nature, to anything at all? What is my penetration factor at center? Intrinsically, am I built closed to the world, or wide, wide open?

This crucial question isn't to be answered lightly from hearsay, or from memory or by means of discursive or speculative thinking, but by simply looking to see. By attending to the present evidence.

I'm taking in this piece of white paper and these black marks appearing on it. Am I experiencing myself as a solid, opaque, limited observing thing here looking across a gap at a solid, opaque, limited observed thing over there? Or am I, on the contrary, no-thing here but room for that thing, with no perceptible distance to keep us apart? In other words, can I conjure up anything here to get in the way of that black-and-white pattern? Am I in receipt of news about that pattern, do I infer or distantly detect it? Or am I invaded by it?

My answer is unhesitating. I'm penetrated, taken over, replaced by that pattern. Is the same now true for you? Are you, too, built open? On this matter you are the sole and final authority.

While agreeing, perhaps, that you are in exactly the same wide-open condition as I am, you may still reasonably object that this has little obvious connection with tenderheartedness. Taking your point, I turn from this page to the nearest face — it could be your face — attending carefully to the situation as it presents itself at this moment. Are we face-to-face, in symmetrical relationship, object confronting object, each shutting out the other? Quite the contrary. Here where I am is no face, no speck of anything to ward you off with, to resist your invasion. Whether I like it or not, I'm so wide open to you that your face is mine and I have no other.

Nor is this a superficial, casual, insignificant coming together. It is an intimacy which is the paradigm of all intimacy, infinitely deep and total, and immensely satisfying — *once I have the humility and the courage to notice it*. The awareness is crucial. I am fully conscious of the perfect way you give me your face, of the perfect way I take it. The way I'm shaped and colored by that fascinating terrain amazes and delights me. Without fuss or comment or conditions you supply my lack, and I have no way of refusing. I can only pretend to refuse you entry.

You could well object that this is all very fine, but you and I could still be at loggerheads, not now in any physical sense but in respect of what really matters — our feelings about each other, our contrasting goals, opinions, life styles. And certainly it is true that simply seeing that I am empty for you now, your face to my no-face, is not enough to ensure a beautiful relationship.

But I do thereby lay a sound foundation for such a relationship. Without this basis of honest, verifiable fact, the superstructure of our relationship is shaky indeed. When I deny our asymmetry — refusing to see the obvious fact that I disappear in your favor — then all my dealings with you are somehow spoiled. And no wonder. Underlying them is the fiction that I'm tough enough to prevent you getting all the way through to me. Our relationship is contaminated — if not doomed — from the start. My perverse habit of confronting your seen face there with my imagined face here is neither sensible nor practical. In fact, this tragically normal abnormality is productive of — and com-pounded of — my fear of you and my hate and my deep anxiety. It's an unkind notice I'm serving on you: "Keep out, I've got one of my own and I much prefer it to yours. Keep yourself to yourself and don't dare to invade my privacy." Vain protestations! Viewing you now in all inno-cence, just as you are given and without explaining anything away, I AM YOU!

But you may well ask me whether I *feel* tender towards you, just because I've had to let you in. Sometimes we feel anything but loving towards the guests we have opened our front door to.

Of course it's true that the *feeling* of warmly welcoming this visitor into my space doesn't immediately and automatically follow from the *fact* that I can't exclude him anyway. The actual experience of tender-ness can't be had just by noticing how penetrable one is. But it's a good start.

And, in my experience, indispensable. It's no use trying to get the feeling of tenderness by itself, while denying the fact that I'm built for it. The feeling so achieved, the feeling without the seeing, the feeling that bases itself on the illusory face-to-face setup, isn't merely hard to come by and harder to maintain: it is phony. It's like protesting fond love for you on the doorstep so long as you don't dare set foot inside. On the other hand, if I consciously let you in (I've no choice, of course) whether currently I feel loving or not, then there's an excellent chance of my love coming to the surface and finding appropriate expression at the right time. Indoors here, I am perfectly placed for explicit loving, because the very act of admitting you was already implicit loving: just as my pretence of holding you there, shivering on my doorstep, was already implicit fear of you and hatred and rejection, and liable to lead to explicit acts of fear and hate and rejection. In short, my recognition that I'm tender by nature, without a trace of toughness, is the very best way (I would say the only way) to cultivate the feeling of tenderness.

This is for testing, not for taking on trust. In day-to-day practice do I find myself loving you more truly, understanding you, caring for you, when I take the trouble to notice that in fact I'm built for loving, understanding, caring?

Yes. This way does work. Consciously admitting you to my space here at once serves to make you more interesting, even fascinating, just as you are. And, on the whole, more lovable. The keen attention you get from me is in any case a sort of affection, and it casts a new and brighter light on all that you are. The ticket of admission highlights and transforms positively the admitted one. Conversely, the refusal of a ticket obscures and transforms him negatively. Everything in the universe looks different and feels different and — damn it, or rather bless it! — is different when I let it right in.

As a child I was very easily moved to tears. I was a softie, not a toughie. I remember one of my schoolmates changing my name from Harding to Softing. I felt deeply ashamed. It was a just comment. Alas, I agreed that I was much too vulnerable, too soft and sentimental. Accordingly (and this is no doubt a typical male response), I pulled a hard face, assuming a tough exterior that began as a pathetic make-believe and became at length capable of taking in strangers, if hardly friends. Of course it was an armor with no substance, a shell of pretence, a thick hide in appearance only, a protection that protected nothing. Primarily it took the form of hallucinating here on these shoulders the countenance that never was here, this misplaced self-image, this fictitious Block at the very center of my universe, obliterating its marvelous clarity and vividness. The result was as painful as it was unlovely. And no wonder. Throwing such a spanner into the middle of the cosmic works, how could I fail to find them seizing up?

I think I was rather less successful than most men in maintaining the fiction of a nuclear thing right here at the center of my world. My self-petrifaction was a singularly feeble enterprise. All the same I managed, in the course of my twenties and early thirties, to construct a flimsy facade to live behind. Less and less was I moved to tears. Men don't cry, and — God help me! — I am a man and not a woman or a crybaby! The incident of the old lady and the kind boy, though it belonged to this very difficult period of my life, was untypical of it. The barriers I was so busy erecting against tenderness were beginning to stand up. I grew more and more like one of those crabs with soft bodies, and a lovely hard whelk-shell to tuck its tenderness into.

But then, at thirty-four, I happened to notice that the shell was quite imaginary. I saw that I was defenseless. In fact, a wonderful combination of absolute vulnerability and absolute safety, for the No-thing at my core presents nothing to be hurt or destroyed. The result of this astounding yet perfectly obvious discovery was that my supposedly too-open nature was no longer shaming but hugely reassuring, relaxing, anxiety-removing. And thereafter, as I got more and more used to being No-thing, I found that occasions of great tenderness were becoming commoner, till all my dealings with people and animals and plants, and even inanimate objects, began to be colored with something of this melting mood, this quality of unshed tears. This isn't sentimentality. It's a way of life based on how it really is. You could call it the way of tenderness.

In my own case, then, the discovery of my true identity or intrinsic nature, of the truth that I'm no tougher than a vacuum, has served to arrest and reverse the hardening of my heart. I recommend this recipe to others. Practice seeing Who you really are and test whether this One is indeed love itself. Not that I promise any quick or very obvious results. The rewards of this practice may seem very meager and tardy, but that is because it runs so deep. Be assured that, insofar as you see that you have no defense against invasion, you will cease to obstruct the love that is natural to you.

Tenderness is as native to you and me as breathing is, and no more to be cultivated. All we have to do is to keep on getting out of its way. We must not lose sight of the fact that while in respect of clearness and preciousness we are diamond-like, in respect of hardness we are the very opposite of diamond-like.

In this resolute refusal to lie to myself about myself rests the secret of my loving, and also of my ultimate security and survival. Only when I imagine you are getting *part* of the way in to me can you seem to damage or destroy me. *Total* invasion ensures there's nothing left here to injure. Thus I am at center no-thing and all things. Right here is at once the incomparable safety and the incomparable expansion, where losing my little self I gain the whole world.

This big and truly sacred heart has many surprises. Here is a concluding instance. I was invited to lecture to a conference of more-or-less committed Buddhists near London, one hundred-fifty of them. The subject was my own somewhat unusual approach to Zen. The lecture seemed to go off fairly well: the audience halfway convinced, but waiting to see which way the cat jumped. Well, the lecturer who followed me enjoyed a reputation as a European authority on Buddhism in general and Zen in particular. His theme was the bogus Zen of certain Westerners who had neither studied in Japan nor undergone the long and severe discipline of sitting meditation and koan solving under an accredited Roshi there, nor received his *inka* or certificate of enlightenment. (Incidentally, he hadn't done any of these things either.) Without actually naming me, he assured those Buddhists that the previous lecture — mine — had little to do with the real Zen, and anyway made no sense. Manifestly I did have a head on my (now sagging) shoulders, and the space there was quite imaginary. Such was my eagerly anticipated debut as a Buddhist teacher, and such was its outcome. I was much worse than a flop. I was a fraud, and I didn't like it at all.

An hour or so after this public "exposure" I found myself walking bemusedly through the now deserted conference hall, and my detractor walking towards me. I still have no idea how it happened but we just fell into each other's arms, embraced for a few moments, and parted. It wasn't the sort of thing I was in the habit of doing at that time, even with my best friends, and certainly he was the kind of Englishman who is least likely to indulge in any such familiarity. Not a word was spoken. Though we have run into each other occasionally since that time, we have never referred to or hinted at that exhibition of tenderness. So far as I know he is just as critical — or contemptuous — of my understanding of the essence of Zen (and its doctrine of one's Original Face which is faceless) as ever he was. I believe that he still, with no personal rancor, considers me to be a not-altogether-harmless eccentric who leads astray genuine inquirers into Eastern religious disciplines.

We have exchanged perhaps no more than twenty polite words since that first meeting. All the same, our relationship will never recover from that moment of sublime tenderness, which said nothing and meant everything, which celebrated nothing less than our everlasting identity at root. In all seriousness I say to him now, as I did silently in that conference hall years ago, I AM YOU, I AM YOU!

BEING
AND
DOING

L ife has a distressing way of presenting us with dilemmas, with seemingly insoluble problems about what to do and what not to do. Not so much problems with no answer as predicaments with two quite contradictory answers. We don't know where we stand. Issues aren't clear-cut. Right and wrong have a tendency to change places. You might say that life is a cleft stick, a game impossible to win, a continuing choice of evils.

One of the most troublesome of these dilemmas is whether to watch or to play the game of life, whether to decline or welcome responsibility, whether to cop out or to cop in.

The world's great teachers don't make it any easier for us to decide. They seem only to add to the confusion. Take Jesus for example. On the one hand, in his Sermon on the Mount, he tells us to relax, to let tomorrow take care of itself, to leave everything to the hidden Power that makes the lilies grow and accounts for their beauty. On the other hand, in the Parable of the Talents, he heaps praise on the busy, duty-bound, responsible citizen, and cheerfully consigns the unprofitable layabout to hell. Or take Nisargadatta: "As long as you have the idea of influencing events, liberation is not for you. The very notion of doership, of being a cause, is bondage." And yet, again and again, he insists that conscious effort is essential in life, and indeed that earnestness is the decisive factor. Finally, take Ramana: "No-one succeeds without effort," he declares. "The successful few owe their success to their perseverance." And then immediately he adds: "A passenger in a train would be silly to keep his load on his head. Let him put it down. He will find that the load reaches the destination all the same. Similarly, let us not pose as the doers, but resign ourselves to the guiding Power."

Well, which shall we do — carry our load or dump it? Help others to carry their loads, or accept no responsibility for them either?

The dilemma is far from being a merely intellectual puzzle. It is real and it hurts, so much so that some of us are being torn apart by it. There is no "right" choice. Whether we take the way of just letting things happen, or of strenuous intervention, we are in for trouble. The life of the dropout who exerts no effort and makes no decisions and accepts no responsibility for himself — let alone for others — what sort of life is that? As for his opposite, the "square" — the hard-working, conscientious, load-carrying, public-spirited fellow — we all know the stresses and strains, the compromises and frustrations and anxieties that are coming to him. To say nothing of the decay and death that will too soon terminate himself and his best-laid plans.

So much for the dilemma that confronts all humans. Now for its resolution. Yes, there is a resolution, a truly practical one that we can immediately start to apply in our everyday living. But first let's be clear about who it is that is engaged in that everyday living.

It is the very nature of every living thing to look after itself, to see to its own welfare, to prefer itself to others. It has no time for altruism. Its job is the survival of its separate thinghood. Thus it lays claim to a portion of the world's space, filling out this volume to the exclusion of all rivals. It has room only for those things that it needs to unthing and incorporate — in a word, for its food. In general, its behavior is aimed at its own survival at others' expense. Now this unrelenting self-seeking is more than a necessity of life. It is the life-thrust itself. Well aware of this, you don't say of an undersized cabbage in your vegetable garden that it generously takes less than its full share of water and sunlight, or praise the weakest piglet in the litter for not being greedy at the trough. On the contrary, you dismiss them as unhealthy, insufficiently alive. It's the same in your flower garden. The finest lilies are those that grab their full share, or more, of the available nutrients.

It's no different with people. Let's face it: a vital, truly alive man is one who knows what he wants, and goes after it, and gets it. He is self-reliant, energetic, audacious, determined, fully cooperative when it suits his purpose, of course, but at other times quite ruthless. Above all, he doesn't sit around moaning about his bad luck, his crippling circumstances, or what God and his parents and his genes and chromosomes did to him. Instead, he takes himself for better or worse as his own property, for which he alone is responsible. And insofar as he avoids this responsibility, and lacks purpose and drive and a strong sense of doership, he falls short of manhood. You could charitably call him a retiring, humble, self-effacing man; or, more honestly, a tired man, a sick man, a failed man, and no more deserving of our admiration than the wilting plant or the undersized animal. To be manly is to take responsibility for one's particular portion of the world and all the life in it, and to live out that life zestfully, without apologies or holding back.

What price, then, the Sermon on the Mount, with its insistence on passivity? And what shall we say of the Saint or the Sage who is happy to stand on the bank of the river of life, watching the waters rush by, and careful not to get his feet wet?

Are the Liberated, in fact, idle, feeble, failed, irresponsible humans? Obviously not. Quite the contrary, they are specially alive and in their own way marvelously determined and energetic and — where necessary — quite ruthless. The Blessed Angela of Foligno, a true Seer of the indwelling God, went so far as to view with almost murderous satisfaction the deaths of her mother and husband and children, whom she regarded as "impediments" to her spiritual life. Young Ramana stole money to go off and live the holy life — a life that throughout relied on others' earnings — and for years he never revealed his whereabouts to his grieving mother. The real Sage or Saint or Seer is a tough and determined character. There is a world of difference between the dropout and the Seer, no matter how alike their appearance and behavior (and sometimes their account of themselves) may happen to be.

And the difference is this: the dropout thinks he is essentially some kind of person (for example a carefree and unconventional person) whereas the Seer sees that he's not a person at all. The one imagines he's a thing in the world, while the other perceives he's the No-thing that contains the world. The one identifies himself with his appearance as a second/third person, the other with his reality as First Person. And not only is the Seer the Space in which things happen, but also the Space in which *all the dilemmas and contradictions that afflict things* happen, without affecting the Space in the slightest. In his capacity as the Container of things, as the Aware Space which is also their Source and Reality, he is himself the reconciliation of whatever divides them.

Thus the Seer resolves the dilemma of passivity versus activity, of detachment versus involvement, of witnessing versus responsibility, in the only way they can be solved — by being the Source of both. As their single Source and Spring, he is upstream of all its bifurcating tributaries. He is the Stem of the cleft stick. He is the indivisible Divider.

And what you, dear reader, really, really are is that Source, that Spring, that Stem. Only in appearance have you ever been human. Intrinsically, therefore, you are free of all the contradictions and tearings apart that humans are subject to.

What is a human being? It is, as we have already noticed, a something — opaque, colored, solid, small. It is full of itself. It occupies and packs out with flesh and blood a few thousand cubic inches, thus excluding other creatures from that volume. It exists by closing itself to others, by being distant from them, distinct from them. *It survives by disappearing them.* It proclaims itself alone, announcing to an alien world: "Here am I! Keep off! No entry!"

Are you like this, in your own experience at this moment?

If so, how do you manage so easily to take in this page and all the printing on it, right now? How else but by giving it room, by disappearing in its favor? Have you anything where you are, at this moment, to keep it out with? Aren't you built open, an empty vessel for filling with anything and everything that may present itself, all the way from the stars to these black marks on paper? And when you look up from this page to the face of your friend over there, don't you take in and take on that face?

Or, if you disagree, if you aren't accommodation for things, but just one of them, how do you account for their brilliance at this moment compared with the obscurity of their observer, not to mention his absence? All you need to settle these crucial questions is to stop thinking long enough just to take a look. And then, if you really do experience yourself as that object you keep on seeing over there in your mirror, if you really are what you look like to others, why then you are a human being after all, and that's that. But if, on the contrary, you really are what you look like to yourself — namely, Room for things to come and go in — why then you are divine, and should put an end to this charade, this pretence of being "only human after all."

As Divinity itself, as the Space for all and the Source of all, you are responsible for all. There is no second Power. Who you really, really are did it all, is doing it all. But notice whether this Space that you are is *efforting* its contents. Do you, who are attending to the scene, have any sense of intending it, of contriving it and cobbling it together, of causing and maintaining it? It is for you, who are responsible for it, to say. Isn't it rather that everything flows spontaneously, without motive or taking thought, from your Being, a ceaseless spin-off from Who you are? Wasn't Ramana right when he said: "No motive can be attributed to that Power ... God is untouched by activities, which take place in His presence?"

Here, then, is the perfect reconciliation between the detachment that witnesses all and the attachment that is involved in all. It was the false notion that you are really a human being that gave rise to the dilemma, the contradiction between the Sermon on the Mount and the Parable of the Talents. At the highest level Dilemma, which is uncomfortable, gives way to Paradox, which isn't. Your true Nature is the Paradox to take care of all paradoxes: there is nothing that is not you and nothing that is you; the Aware Space is and isn't its contents; you care and you don't care; you control things and they just happen. This may sound silly, but in fact it is the perfection of wisdom. Also it works.

And even at less exalted levels these conclusions make sense. The responsibility that a man feels, his sense of controlling this and that, is illusory. Every event in his life is conditioned by the other events constituting the universe, as if everybody were making a living by taking in everybody else's washing. Attributing particular causes to particular events, and feeling personally responsible for any of them, is unrealistic. The universe is strictly indivisible, and the only way to take responsibility for some of it is to take responsibility for all of it. Which is to be the Whole of it.

You as the Whole of you are responsible for everything, and manage it all very well — and this without any sense of responsibility or good management. How can you know this for sure? Only by being yourself now and consulting your firsthand experience. Only by ceasing to masquerade as a man, a woman, or a child.

The answer to the dilemma of being and doing, to the problem of personal responsibility, is not to give up the feeling of being personally responsible for this and that, but to take it to the limit — where it vanishes, and you can say with Ramana Maharshi:

- Action forms no bondage. Bondage is the false notion: "I am the doer."
- Be fixed in the Self and act according to nature

SOPHIA'S
THREE
SUITORS

There once lived a princess called Sophia, who was not only charming and incomparably beautiful, but also (true to her name) the very perfection of wisdom. One day, three suitors arrived at her palace — a brave knight, a love-struck poet, and a rude swineherd.

First, the knight was admitted to her presence.

"How many dragons have you killed recently?" inquired the princess.

"Practically none, dear lady," he admitted. "But my sword and armor are of the finest steel, and for love of you I am going to search out and slay every dragon in this land. I realize the immensity of this task, of course. For these monsters hide in the depths of the sea and in dark and tortuous caves, and will have to be tracked down one by one and enticed into the open air, where I shall finish them off. But however long it takes I vow to accomplish this quest, and so at last become worthy of you. All I ask, before setting out, is your favor and your blessing."

"Indeed you have them, brave knight," exclaimed the princess. "Your determination and courage are beyond praise, and those terrible dragons certainly have to be dealt with."

So the knight rode away, full of happy anticipation, his armor flashing in the sunlight.

Next, the poet was shown in to the audience chamber, and began humbly to plead his suit.

"All I can offer, dear princess, is my adoration and the poor songs it inspires. I only hope that one day my devotion to you — expressed, perhaps, in some great composition worthy of its subject — will win your heart. Meanwhile, I beg to be allowed to remain here. Unlike that knight — does he really love you? — I cannot bear to be far away from your presence. Should you grant it, I promise not to take advantage of this boon, and come too near you."

"Dear poet," replied the princess tenderly, "I value your devotion more than I can say, and it is true that no one wins me who is cold and halfhearted. I shall give orders that you are given a pleasant room in the palace, from whose windows you will sometimes be able to see me walking in the rosegarden."

As soon as the poet, delighted and grateful, had gone to his new quarters, the swineherd was admitted, by extremely reluctant officials, to the royal presence. He was an uncouth young man, illiterate, ragged, and still smelling of the pigsty.

"I want you and nothing else," he blurted out, "and I want you now."

"But this is outrageous," cried the princess. "The brave knight and the devoted poet dedicate their lives to deserving me one day, and here are you, a malodorous rustic, demanding me instantly, as if I were your property, yours for the asking."

"Why so you are," retorted the swineherd, unabashed.

"I'll have you thrown out," cried the furious princess. "I'm not sure I won't have you thrown into a dungeon."

"Before you do that," he replied, "let me tell you something. Your knight is in love with chivalry and dragon hunting, and that's why he's happy to wait for you indefinitely. As for your poet, he's in love with love and his own love-poems, and that's why he promises to keep a respectful distance. The truth is that both are frightened of you. But true love casts out fear, and I'm not frightened of you, and I claim you right away."

"I insist those horrible dragons are dealt with," cried the princess, stamping her foot. "Though you may not be frightened of me, it seems you cannot face them."

"To the knight who faces them out there, they look terrifying, and are in fact practically invulnerable. That's the way he likes his dragons. But when I take them in the rear they become mere pussycats. Now that I've come to live with you these monsters will turn into our household pets, though it may take years to domesticate them all."

"For a swineherd you are quite intelligent," conceded the princess, "but I still require the wholehearted devotion that the poet offers, even if his good manners are beyond you."

"The devotion I offer is inseparable from union. Already we are one, and your infinite perfections are more than enough for both of us."

"Ah well," sighed the princess, "it seems I have no alternative. Marry me now, rude swineherd, and deserve me later."

"As my true self — as you, heart of my heart — how could I deserve myself? And as my false self, as that somewhat smelly rustic, how could I deserve anything at all, even if I killed a thousand dragons or wrote the love-poem of all time?"

"All the same," replied the princess, now smiling broadly, "there is room for considerable improvement. Indeed I observe that it has begun already. Even that horrid smell has almost gone."

RAMANA MAHARSHI
AND
J. KRISHNAMURTI

Spiritually minded people have a way of blurring the distinctions between one master and another. They are really teaching the same thing (we are told) but in very different tones of voice. This looks like an amiable habit, making for ecumenism and peace in our time, O Lord. Fair enough. But it can be the result of laziness or superficiality, of failure to listen carefully and go deeply into what's being said, of fudging boundaries when what's needed is clear and sharp discrimination.

Really, to follow a spiritual path to its conclusion, you have to be careful not to be diverted along other paths. To change the metaphor, if you want to enjoy the full flavor of any spiritual fare, you won't blend it with other spiritual fares till the concoction is so bland it's flavorless.

Take for example the teaching of Ramana Maharshi on the one hand, and of Krishnamurti on the other. Some of their respective followers or disciples or devotees tell me that they are saying the same thing, couched in very different languages. I can't agree. I find great differences of substance, and not merely of style, between their teachings. This chapter outlines some of the more important ones.

But let's not begin with points of disagreement but points of agreement. Both Ramana Maharshi and Krishnamurti insist that the answer to the problems of life is to be found within, that deep inside us lies all we need. In this, of course, they are in line with all real sages and seers.

So far so good. Now we come to the differences, or, if you like, the disagreements.

It is essential, says Krishnamurti, to understand ourselves, how we think, what we think, why we think that way, the nature of our conditioning. "To follow oneself, to see how one's thought operates, one has to be extraordinarily alert, so that as one begins to be more and more alert to the intricacies of one's own thinking and responses and feelings, one begins to have a greater awareness, not only of oneself but of another with whom one is in relationship." Everywhere Krishnamurti insists that we must get to know the processes of the mind.

Ramana Maharshi flatly denies that there is a mind to get to know. On investigation "it will be found that the mind does not exist." "There is nothing but the Self. To inhere in the Self is the thing. Never mind the mind. If its source is sought, it will vanish."

Very similar is the counsel of Nisargadatta Maharaj: "It is the mind that tells you that the mind is there. Don't be deceived. It is the bland refusal to consider the convolutions and convulsions of the mind that can take you beyond it."

A thorough search of the talks of Maharshi and Krishnamurti would no doubt yield passages that would tone down the blatant differences between them on this score — in theory. But in practice it's irreducible. Either you go baldheaded for Who you really are, or else you get to work on all that mental stuff which is alleged to block the vision of that Who. They just won't mix, and there's no sense in jumping back and forth from one to the other.

The question at issue is whether that blessed vision is available right now and just as we are, or only after a long, perhaps lifelong preparation.

Here is Krishnamurti on this topic: "Before we can find out what the end-purpose of life is, what it all means, we must begin with ourselves, must we not? It sounds so simple, but it is *extremely* difficult [K's italics]. The difficulty is that we are so impatient; we want to get on, we want to reach an end, and so we have neither the time nor the occasion to give ourselves the opportunity to study, to observe."

For total contrast, listen to Maharshi: "There is nothing so simple as being the Self. It requires no effort, no aid. All are seeing God always, but they don't know it. I see what needs to be seen. I see only just what all see, nothing more. The Self is always self-evident."

There are other notable differences.

For Krishnamurti the great scriptures of the world are so many man-traps. How he can be sure of this is an interesting question, since he makes a point of never reading them. Equally, gurus imprison us in their systems. He himself is not a guru, he insists. Here's another interesting question: if he isn't "a revered spiritual teacher" (which is a pretty fair definition of a guru) what on Earth is he? Anyway — guru, nonguru, or antiguru — the practice he advocates, of approaching Self-knowledge by studying the movements of your mind, is certainly a very gradual one, in which you never catch up with yourself. "The more you know yourself, the more clarity there is. Self-knowledge has no end — you don't come to an achievement, you don't come to a conclusion. It is an endless river."

How different is Maharshi's way! He has read the scriptures, and recognizes that their study can stimulate Self-enquiry, no less than (alas!) serve as a substitute for Self-enquiry. Also he stresses the importance of the true Guru within you. You are strongly urged to see directly into your Nature. But if you imagine you can't do so (more truly, if you won't do so) then surrender to a guru who will help to remove the obstruction to your seeing. In other words, you have the choice of the short path of Self-enquiry, or the longer path of Devotion, leading to the goal of Self-realization. But, whichever path you take, the Vision it leads to is by no means a matter of degrees or stages. It's all-or-nothing, sudden, complete, perfect. While time and practice are needed, as a rule, to establish Self-realization, they add nothing to the experience. They habituate it, so that it's no longer occasional or intermittent. Also they allow it to take effect in all the areas and levels of one's life. The Self can't be partially seen, much less mis-seen. Why? Because it's the Self that sees the Self, and certainly not a human being as such that does so.

I think it will help at this stage to move on from the differences between two particular teachers to more general considerations.

In surveying spirituality East and West, two temperaments, two types of teachers and doctrines, can be discerned. The gulf between them is wide and deep. For the first kind, Reality or the Goal (which terms they would probably not capitalize) is strictly impersonal, a mere absence rather than an awesome Presence, a nothing whatsoever rather than the marvelous No-thing that's wide awake to Itself as Nothing — Everything, a void that's so void it's void even of voidness, an unmystery, a disappearance. There's no self, let alone a Self.

For the second temperament Reality is the diametric opposite of all this. The Self alone is quite real, suprapersonal and by no means impersonal, altogether adorable and marvelous and unspeakably mysterious, *ananda* (bliss) no less than *sat* (being) and *chit* (awareness). No wonder people of this persuasion delight in bandying the word GOD, which for the former sort is the dirtiest of words. And of course there are those who go on to talk of a God who is Love itself, of the One who gives his very life for his world, who disappears in favor of — yes, of you and of me.

In the interest of brevity rather than accuracy, you could label the first type spiritual-psychological and the second spiritual-religious. Of course there are all sorts of intermediate positions between these polar opposites, and even attempts to bridge the gulf that parts them. But the gulf remains.

It's pretty obvious on which side of the gulf Maharshi belongs, and on which side Krishnamurti belongs. And, for that matter, on which side I find myself. If you press me hard enough I'll admit that it's temperament — or let's say my very Christian conditioning as a young child — that lands me on the spiritual-religious slope of the Great Gulf and that the case I put up for that side is ex post facto: I keep finding reasons for what I believe on instinct, anyway.

Happily, however, that's not quite the end of the story. When you and I, *whatever our temperamental differences,* turn the arrow of our attention round 180 degrees, What we see within is one and the same for us both and absolutely unconditioned. How can we be so sure? For the reason that here, at the very bottom of the valley where the two sides of the Gulf come together, there's nothing left to disagree about. Here, all disciples of Maharshi, of Krishnamurti, of any teacher or no teacher are free to share the essential realization that unites us all eternally.

And here, at last, is to be found the true ecumenism that heals without any fudging or blurring of distinctions. Here is the ultimate pacification of strife in general, and in particular of religious fanaticism and intolerance. What a simple and universal medicine for this sickness-unto-death is ours — effective, free, abundant, and handier than our right hand!

Let us — you and I — take it right now, and not wait for others. They will follow in God's good time.

ON HAVING
A
HEAD

I beseech you, in the bowels of Christ,
think it possible you may be mistaken.
—OLIVER CROMWELL

I have a tale to tell against myself. A somewhat embarrassing — if not shaming — confession to make.

It happened quite recently, this sudden realization that threatened to undermine the very basis of the work I had been doing and the life I had been living for half a century. Most of this time I had been going round cheerfully pointing out to everybody who would listen that, in one's own firsthand experience of oneself, one lacks a head, and converting not a few to that unusual opinion.

Of course I had quickly added that, in place of the missing head, is a parade of sensations —roughnesses and smoothnesses and tickles and tensions and aches, as well as a great variety of sounds and tastes and smells. Not to mention a maelstrom of thoughts and feelings. Nevertheless (I insisted) the contrast between the loose and ever-changing parade of events strung out in time that belong on *these* shoulders and the tight and stable pattern of colored shapes all packed together in space that belong on *those* shoulders couldn't be more striking. So much so that I got into the habit of looking in my mirror to see what I was *not* like, and asking myself whether what I was looking out of had *anything* in common with what I was looking at.

Accordingly I concluded that, whatever it is that lurks here at the center of my world, it is certainly not a *head* — if that word is to mean anything at all — and I'm indeed headless.

This self-portrait will indicate what I mean by headlessness.

It aims to show how, when I try to get hold of my lost head, I lose my hands as well. How what I'm looking out of isn't so much a thing as an antithing, a searching and universal solvent, a flame that, while it lights up everything that keeps its distance, burns up everything that ventures too near. And my purpose, throughout this past half-century, has been to tend this flame and spread its light.

Well, there you have it — the background of the story I have to tell.

That was how matters stood as recently as three months ago. And then, for no reason I know of, it suddenly occurred to me that *a man born blind, fingering one of his hands and then his head, has as much reason for believing in the latter as in the former.*

Please check this for yourself right now. Go blind (that's to say, close your eyes), handle your left hand with your right, then your left arm and shoulder, your neck, and finally your head — back, sides, and front, all over ... Isn't the present evidence for your head just as convincing as for your hand? For a head, moreover, which is as firmly attached to your trunk as your hand is to your arm.

Now let's admit it, a fundamental truth that's untrue for a blind man isn't a fundamental truth at all. It doesn't deserve to be taken seriously. And certainly it's no foundation for building a life on.

So I found myself asking myself some awkward questions. What if, all through those years of dedicated endeavor, I had been mistaken? Or worse, had more or less unconsciously suppressed vital evidence, cooking the books in favor of a cherished theory, not to say obsession?

Could it be that — more hidden from me than from others — my stratagem for reversing my feelings of inferiority and getting noticed at any price, for hoisting myself head and shoulders above the masses, had been to pretend I *lacked* head and shoulders? How's that for irony?

I tell you I was shocked. Not tumbled, but shaken.

The shock was somewhat cushioned by three considerations. The first was that, many times in my life, a serious setback or looming disaster has issued in something new and wonderful, a valuable realization, an opening out of new vistas. This man's extremity, as they say, has so often turned out to be God's opportunity that my hope was that history would obligingly repeat itself yet once more. The second consideration was that, over many years, the experience and practice of headlessness has made a profound difference for the better in many lives no less than in my own, and what works so well and for so long and for so many is unlikely to be the nonsense or the lie it might appear to be. The third consideration was (or rather *is*) that right now as I type these words on this sheet of paper I can find nothing here on my shoulders to keep it out with, absolutely nothing in its way. Everything I see decapitates me.

All the same, here was a real challenge, a hiatus, an important piece missing from the jigsaw of my life and work. Clearly I had a duty to myself and others to find, if I could, the missing piece and put it on display — better late than never.

Obviously my first job was to investigate yet again what exactly it is that I'm fingering here in the place I'm looking out of. I decided to examine, more carefully than ever before, this home-base of mine, and, coming to my senses afresh, to rely throughout on what they might reveal, on the clearly *given*. This meant abandoning my most cherished convictions about headlessness and all that, and starting all over again, aided by whatever new experiments seemed promising.

At once a bunch of indubitable facts came to light. I do — yes, I do after all — have a something here on my shoulders, a topknot or finial, and the only fitting name for the thing is a *head* of some sort. Of what sort? Well, it's the head (furnished with all the normal protuberances and hollows and apertures) of a living creature. And not just any living creature but a human one. And not just any human, but a special one: all sorts of peculiarities identify it as Douglas Harding's alone. And it's of a piece with the rest of his body. Though manifesting itself to me after its own fashion and on its own terms, it's just as real as any other part of my body. And though for me the head I'm looking out of is as transparent as the window I happen also to be looking out of at this moment, it's as solid and as actual-factual as the glass in that window. To deny this would be to descend to the intellectual level of the blue-bottle hurling itself again and again against the glass.

"All quite obvious and normal," I can hear you commenting dryly, "and surprising only to no-head addicts."

So be it — thus far. But here's where the abnormalities and surprises take off, and there emerges a whole series of startling facts about this real head of mine, and just how wildly different it is from all the other heads I've come across: including, of course, the head in my mirror.

For a start I notice that, though the same way up as those heads over there, it's attached to a body that's the other way up. This means that just below shoulder level I FOLD, as this page you are reading folds with the page opposite. Fold, I find, to breaking point.

Is the same true for you? Please make sure by holding up your forearm like this

Here the scene fades upwards

(a)

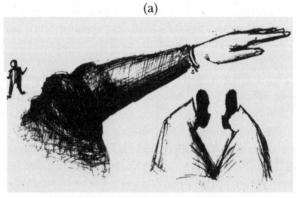

(b)

Here the scene fades downwards

and bringing it slowly down from (a) at the top of the scene where the sky (or the ceiling if you are indoors) fades away downwards. Notice how the rest of your body, in contrast to that of the little man in the distance, is upside-down. His feet — like the feet of the person in your mirror — are underneath him, yours are on top.

But your *head* is the same way up as his. It isn't upside-down. Please make sure of this by repeating the experiment with your forearm held closer, so that your forefinger just grazes your truly huge profile — your forehead at (a), then your nose and chin, and finally your neck at (b).

To have a head that's as clear as glass is wonderful. To have a head that folds with its body is wonderful. To have a head that also has room for the world is wonderful indeed. *For in fact this real head of mine, though tangibly featuring my merely human and merely personal hair, forehead, eyebrows, nose, mouth, and so on, is sky-high and worldwide and world-deep, and it features the cosmos itself.* Between your ears a coiffure, between mine a coiffure and the clear light of the morning! What a miraculous coming-to-a-head is here, this most intimate conjunction of the cosmic and the human and the personal and the glasslike impersonal, and in the very place where I insisted I was headless!

I'm not asking you to believe me but to check whether you, too, are built to the same grand and astonishing design. This you do — right now, if you please — by outlining your head with your forefinger, touching in turn your hair, ear, cheek, and chin, all round and back again to where you started. If you are conducting this experiment (or, should I say, going on this world tour?) in the open, so much the better. In any case notice how your real head as so outlined is even larger than the scene. With ease it accommodates whatever happens to be on display, whether it's a sky full of stars, or the dream you are dreaming, or the room you are now sitting in, or the tealeaves in your teacup. And all this without ceasing to be as human and as personal as they come.

To clinch the matter beyond doubt, notice that it's not just your head but the upper part of your body that's so magnificently capacious. Along with those little heads over there go little arms, along with your immense head here go immense arms. Here's how you check this. While looking straight-ahead, spread wide your outstretched arms till they almost disappear from view. Actually do this, and you will see that they *embrace* the world that your head is already taking in and taking on.

What false modesty it is, to deny these undeniable and heartening facts! What a nonsense it is, this prime delusion of man, this belittling and indeed self-mutilating conviction that he *is* what he *looks like* to other men! It's as if the Atlantic were to persuade itself that it's the puddle it looks like from the Moon, or the drop it looks like from beyond the Moon, and neither deep nor wide nor wet nor windswept!

Actually there's no end to the differences between the head that's here and the head that's there — whether it's in my mirror, or on other people's shoulders, or in their cameras. *Differences* is far too mild a word. Glaring discrepancies is nearer the mark. What makes the continual discovery and rediscovery of these discrepancies so crucial is our fatal determination, from childhood onwards, to identify ourselves with that apparent and peripheral head and to dis-identify ourselves with the real and central head it stems from. In a word, our ingrained *wrong-headedness*.

Let's look, briefly, at a sample of seven of these discrepancies, these instances of wrong-headedness. If, like me, you have noticed them before, take a fresh look, and discover that here every time is the first time.

1. This real but mistaken-for-unreal head is constantly and without effort wiping out one collection of things — it may be a constellation, it may be a range of mountain peaks or a stand of trees or a terrace of houses, it may be the furniture in one corner of the room you are sitting in — and replacing it by another collection. At will it transmutes anything into something else. But that mistaken-for-real head can't even transmute its little self. It merely turns to the right or the left, poor thing!

2. This real but mistaken-for-unreal head decorates and redecorates the world, suddenly painting it rose-colored, blue, gray, practically any color, at will. But that mistaken-for-real head merely decorates and redecorates its eyeballs with discs of colored glass, poor thing!

3. This real but mistaken-for-unreal head peoples the universe with extraordinary characters, some hilarious, some admirable, many so-so, a few quite horrible. It brings to pass monsters and marvels of every kind, caught up in all sorts of remarkable happenings, in scenery to match. That mistaken-for-real head merely stations itself in front of a wad of paper covered with black marks, fiddling with and staring fixedly at it for hours on end. Or laboriously covers reams of snow-white paper with similar black marks.

4. This real but mistaken-for-unreal head changes the world's disposition from sad to happy to sad, from stormy to calm and back

again, from just about any mood to any other mood. That mistaken-for-real head merely inserts foreign substances — uppers, downers, pep-pills, what-have-you — into a toothed slit near its base, or bends upwards and downwards the curved margins of that slit or slot,

or produces pious noises from that slit or slot. Rarely, it must be added, with complete success.

The Grail Legend, with its tale of a parade of sacred objects in the WasteLand, is very much to the point here. These objects include a severed head. If the knight who witnesses the parade isn't interested enough to ask questions about this head the WasteLand stays waste and its Wounded King stays wounded. The lesson for me is clear. Go deeply into the meaning and truth of this central head of mine and be sure that this research, seemingly so private and ineffectual, has universal repercussions. My true head not only contains the world, but really does determine its state of health. What I see depends on what I am.

5. This real but mistaken-for-unreal head is all the time moving mountains, hills, houses, trees, you name it, shifting them around effortlessly.

Don't believe me. Try it out for yourself. Exercising this miraculous faculty of cosmic telekinesis, you can increase or decrease the distance between that house opposite and the tree in its garden, or shift that chair nearer to or further away from the door. And so on and on. Whereas that mistaken-for-real head, swaying from side to side, shifts only itself.

6. Most impressive and neglected of all, this real but mistaken-for-unreal head regularly creates and destroys the world. Whereas that mistaken-for-real head merely raises and lowers a couple of hair-fringed flaps attached to its surface. As for the poor little head in my mirror, why it can't even do that!

7. Strangely enough, the exercise of the six foregoing powers — and

by God they are not to be sniffed at — leaves one's real head any-thing but big-headed in the pejorative sense of that term. You could say it's the acme of modesty and unobtrusiveness, humbler than humble. Why so? Because it's continually abolishing itself, *vanishing without trace in favor of other heads*. Its proper business, its very nature is to make way for and give place to all comers, however troublesome or dull they happen to be. Essentially self-effacing, this original face of mine is faceless, this original head is headless. Conversely, that acquired and mistaken-for-real head is nothing if not heady, and it is manifestly closed to all comers. Its proper business is to insist on itself. It has no room for anything else.

For the purpose of our enquiry this seventh discrepancy is the crucial one.

It's time to take stock.

In a sense I have to admit that headless is precisely what I'm *not*, and that in promoting headlessness for the past half-century I couldn't have been more mistaken. Securely mounted on these broadest of shoulders, larger than life and twice as natural, is my only real, indispensable, living head, my very own superhuman and human and personal head.

But in another and far truer sense I wasn't wrong after all, and every moment of that long dedication to headlessness was time well spent. Exercising the last and surely most wonderful of the powers we have just been sampling, this truly headed one here is truly headless. Its crowning power and glory is that it surrenders all power and glory, gives itself away leaving no residue, gives all it has and is to the world that sorely needs just that. Helen's face, they say, launched a thousand ships. My face, *when I let go of it*, launches a thousand worlds.

So it turns out that none of these discoveries about my true or superhead subtract one iota from my long experience of headlessness, or invalidate It for a moment. Quite the contrary, they confirm and enrich and enliven that experience, which I can now describe as a head-lessness that is born unceasingly of headfulness. No risk now of this central emptiness reading as a dead and dreary emptiness, a mere void, a nothing, a static absence. It's a verb rather than a noun, an ever-renewed absenting. And after all this makes good sense: only what's full can empty itself, only what lives can give its life so that others may live.

Much of this has a familiar ring for me, and maybe for you. What's ever new, what I shall never get used to is the inescapable fact that this wonderful four-tier topknot is mine. It's what I put my Panama hat on! It's none other than the head I shampoo!

What about the blind man whose hand and head seemed to threaten my life's work?

Our discoveries remove that threat. It's true that some of the realizations and powers I have listed — and obviously this includes the *folding* of the visible part of one's body with the tangible part — aren't available to him. Nevertheless a sufficient number remain, and there are others. The one thing (or rather, no-thing) he can clearly see — and there's no other way to see it — is the limitless being that he really, really is. And that is why, all along, I have had no more difficulty sharing this vision with blind people than with sighted people.

As for my suspicion — voiced at the beginning of this chapter — that the threat posed by the blind man concealed a promise, that promise has been fulfilled far more generously than I had imagined possible. Once more the dear Lord has seized the opportunity of this man's extremity to shower him with blessings, blessings superhuman and human and personal and subpersonal — sub everything. Blessings poured upon his head of course — where else? — in accordance with tradition.

Now it would be strange if this good news had up to now passed unnoticed, had never dawned upon the sages and seers whose business throughout three millennia has been radical self-knowledge. And of course there it was, scattered very thinly but very widely over the great spiritual traditions and often expressed obliquely, but plain enough as soon as one knew what to look for.

Jelaluddin Rumi could be called the Apostle of Headlessness, and sure enough it was among the voluminous utterances of this greatest of Sufis that I found the following:

> You have two heads. That head of clay is from earth,
> this pure head is from heaven. That derived head is
> manifest, this original head is hidden.

> It is my business to lose my head, the business of my
> King to give me a new one.

Or take Plotinus, the third-century neo-platonist philosopher:

> To real Being we go back, all that we have and are. To
> This we return as from This we came ... When we look
> outside of This on which we depend, we ignore our
> unity. Looking outward we see many faces, look in-
> ward and all is the One Head. If a man could but be
> turned about — by his own motion or by the happy
> pull of Athene — he would at once see God, and him-
> self, and the All.

According to Zen Buddhism I'm enlightened when I see and consciously live from my "Original Face." The implications are threefold.
First, that I have an Original Head, for a face without a head is no
more real than a Cheshire cat's smile without a Cheshire cat. Second,
that I also have an acquired face and head, for an original face and
head without an acquired one to contrast itself with is a misnomer.
And, third, that to superimpose that acquired face and head over there
in my mirror upon this original one right here is endarkening and
unhealthy, if not plain silly. I conclude that what the realized Zen man
lives from is what the realized Sufi lives from. And it is none other than
what we have been calling here our real and true and truly blessed
head.

Isn't it also what the realized Christian lives from when, following
St. Paul, he experiences Christ as "the head of the body?" Or perhaps,
following St. Augustine, he speaks mysteriously of "the flesh of Christ
which is the head of man?" Of course neither saint is referring to the
historical Jesus who was born and lived and died long ago in that distant land, but to the eternal and cosmic Christ who from the beginning was God and was with God, and by whom all things are created
and sustained. The Christ in me that is more me than me, the heavenly man, the new man, the Word that is forever being made flesh,
forever being spoken. Spoken (please note) with a voice that is at once
divine, and human, and personal — so fleshly-personal that, though I
speak for Him and from Him, I must do so in tones and accents that
are instantly recognizable as those of Douglas Harding alone. Even his
"Hello" on the phone, last heard years ago, is like no other's. There's
personhood for you!

Every creature is a unique divine incarnation. I have long felt that
here, in the mystery of the Word made flesh, of the Ultimate forever
becoming the Intimate — superbly pictured in the Christmas star-to-

manger story — is the master key to true religion, deep healing, lasting joy. I have been sure of it, without being at all clear about the mode of its operation. But now, arriving under the improbable guise of a challenge to my life's mission, what should have been obvious from the start discloses itself. Though the mystery and the wonder of this incarnation remain more and not less mysterious and wonderful, a bright light shines on how it actually comes to pass in my own case, and by extension in all others. It's a perfectly extraordinary four-level descent, and it's going on in the place where I imagined I had a perfectly ordinary one-level head doing its perfectly ordinary levelheaded thing.

Where does this divine descent end? Exactly where does it bottom out? Let's go for the answer to the very first of our discoveries, the one in which we found our real and immense head *folding to breaking point* with our other-way-up little body. The divine descent is completed just below these outstretched arms that embrace the world, in the region of the heart. Not — repeat not — in the region of the cool head but of the warm heart. And the broken heart, at that. Nothing short of that extremity of emptying and self-naughting where I fold and go broke, will, by completing the circle, join the Nothing to the All which is its other aspect. Thank Heaven there's nothing vague or airy-fairy about this lowest but most awesome of places. It's for pinpointing precisely: in fact, it's the spot I naturally point to when indicating myself. It's the nadir where exhalation ends and inhalation begins, and where incarnation becomes excarnation. In Pauline language, it's the place where I am crucified and resurrected with Christ.

Here at last is the true Sacred Heart, the broken heart that heals all heartbreak. Also a warning for those whose hearts are still intact: in particular for anyone who imagines that "losing one's head" is enough, thank you very much. I say that, till the loss of one's head issues in the finding of one's heart — a heart so tender that it is mortally wounded by the world's appalling suffering — till then one falls far short of the goal which is the love that transmutes all suffering. And here a near miss, just because it can so easily be mistaken for a bull's eye, can be *worse than* a mile off target.

No, headlessness is not enough, for the simple reason that it can, by itself, be quite loveless. I have some evidence from others' lives, and plenty from my own, that this is a solemn fact.

Finally, by way of summary and conclusion, I would like to look a little more closely at what "having a head here" amounts to.

1. *This real head of mine is divine.* I can find no other adjective that does justice to its boundlessness, its speckless clarity and nothingness in one direction and its fullness and everythingness in the opposite direction, its ability not just to set in motion and transform the world overall and in detail but to make and unmake it at will — and all of it wide-awake to itself. Now to arrogate all or any of these powers to myself as a human being, and to a particular human being at that, would be as ridiculous as it would be conceited. In my essential functioning I am divine, whether I admit it or not. It is by the way, so to speak, according to the particular form that functioning takes, that I am human and this particular human.

   But it's not as if this real head of mine were divine in part and human in part and personal in part and absent in part, or some explosive mixture of all four ingredients. No, at its own level the divinity is absolute and by no means blurred or diminished by its descent into humanness and personhood and nothingness. Only my uncontaminated Godhood is capable of those primary functions which we have sampled, and which I had either falsely attributed to my manhood or else completely overlooked. Not even the dimmest or foggiest head runs short of divine prowess. To lack divinity is to lack being.

2. *This real head of mine is human: in fact, animal-human.* Amazingly, all these divine functions are going on in a container which, though infinitely capacious, is revealed by touch to be animal-human beyond all doubt. This hairdo, these lobed ears, these hairless cheeks, these oval eyes and peculiar nose and mouth, though distinguishable from those of a gorilla or chimpanzee, clearly belong to the same genus. They are simian, as distinct from feline, canine, and so on. Never was a container so outshone by its contents! And, of course, along with the animal form go countless animal functions such as breathing and eating, and along with the human form go countless human functions — all those modes of feeling and thinking and behaving that characterize *Homo sapiens.* Nevertheless I can find no evidence that my awareness of my divine nature diminishes my animal-human nature. Rather the reverse. They dovetail neatly. Divinity doesn't incarnate tentatively or halfheartedly. It calls nothing common or unclean. It is no snob.

3. *This real head of mine is personal and unique.* Passing my hands again

over its surface, I detect all manner of peculiarities — patches of rough skin, wrinkles, prominences and hollows that belong to Douglas Harding alone. Here, not to be despised is an unimaginably elaborate system of marks — a data-coding, so to say — that sets him apart from all humans that are or were or shall be. Just as the divine stays divine and the human stays human, so the personal stays personal, in spite of its most intimate involvement with other levels. Correction: not *in spite* of that involvement but *because* of it. The linking of our unique personality with the human-in-general and the supervenient divine is in no danger of de-personalizing us. On the contrary, till the human cleaves to the suprahuman divine, and the personal to the suprapersonal divine, they are not yet themselves. You may have noticed how, on the one hand, those folk who are inordinately personal, insisting on their unique selfhood and idiosyncrasies, are unsure of themselves, apt to be slavishly imitative, and in fact scarcely personal at all. And how, on the other hand, those who see that in their divine nature they are one and the same, are of all people the least likely to resemble one another in their human nature and its personal expression. They are unpredictable and nonconformist without any intention of being so.

4. *This real head of mine, as room for other heads, is a no-head* — a fact which it owes solely to is divinity. Only the Highest is humble enough to come all the way down to the lowest. In my human and personal capacity what I most dread is disappearing in favor of others. In my divine capacity it is what I most enjoy. God is love, the love that dies for the world, and when I truly love, it is as Him, and with His love that I do so.

In short, yes, a thousand times yes — I do have a head. But, God Almighty, *what* a head!

MAP 1. FIRST PERSON SINGULAR

Though not to scale and much simplified, this map shows the capital city (so to speak) in the midst of its ring-shaped provinces. That's to say, it distinguishes sharply what I am for myself here at center from what I look like to the observer approaching me from afar. Distinguishes ME, the one central Reality, from my countless regional appearances. Appearances or manifestations astonishingly variegated yet orderly and neatly zoned. The Whole comprising a strictly indivisible unity, each of whose bits and pieces is what it is by virtue of all the other bits and pieces. In no other way than this, as nothing less than this, is one actually served up. Attempting to fragment it is attempting suicide.

Throughout those forty years this map proved an invaluable guide and inspiration leading to all sorts of discoveries, some of them very applicable to everyday living. Here above all was a handy and eloquent reminder of my true and breathtaking identity, telling me how very far I am from being that little human I see in my mirror and others are in receipt of, that eccentric and rusticated provincial. It's no exaggeration to say that this simple sketch — setting out what every schoolchild should know — has done more to alert this person to his first-personhood than all the spiritual-psychological books he has ever read. I recommend it as an alarm clock for waking one from the recurrent nightmare of one's false identity as a mere human — whatever that impossible abstraction could mean.

All the same, it suffers from grave defects.

Notably it represents the capital — the ME — as a mere blob or point, in spite of the fact that, *when visited*, it turns out to be wider than the wide world. As shown, it's not the capital but the provinces which open out and capture our attention. It's as if our map were deliberately designed to discourage excursions to the metropolis, and suggest that a visit would hardly be worth the price of a cheap day ticket. I remember a popular song of the sixties in which the singer complained that, though she had been to New York and Paris and London and lots of other famous capitals, there was one serious omission. "I've never been to ME," was the refrain of her song. If she had been going by our map, she might have added: "And I doubt whether I've missed much." The sad truth is that nearly all of us share that unfavorable opinion. There's a crying need for a revised map which does equal justice to the everywhereness as well as the centrality of ME.

There's another sense in which Map 1 could scarcely be more mis-leading. It portrays my central Reality as the private property and pris-oner of its regional appearances. Here's a ME in a straitjacket, a ME which is mine and only mine, which I hold all round in my iron grasp. If it's amazing, adorable, love-worthy, absolutely unique, and so on, these sublime qualities don't belong to itself as that ever-absconding Subject-Object but rather to myself as this ever-captive Subject-Sub-ject, as this one-hundred percent Self-centered one who doesn't know what Otherness means. Here, for what it's worth, is a Deity that's wholly immanent and stripped bare of every trace of transcendence, all *Atman* and no *Brahman* thank you. One you can cheerfully gobble up for break-fast, dinner, and tea, with not a crumb left over for the birds of heaven. A meal that's apt to leave you with a bad taste in your mouth and hungrier than ever.

If you imagine that this kind of spirituality doesn't exist — or, if it does, isn't for taking seriously — what about these typical excerpts from the *Ashtavakra Gita*, a Hindu scripture highly regarded in some quarters?

Wonderful am I, salutations to Myself!
From Me the world is born, in Me it exists, in Me it dissolves.
All praise be to Me!

An Atmaholic, if ever there was one! But wait a minute. Aren't the following pronouncements, by two of the greatest sages of this century, instances of the same unbridled immanentism?

When there is nothing except Yourself you are happy.
That is the whole truth. — RAMANA MAHARSHI

When you find everything within Yourself and there is nothing other than your own Self, that is full realiza-tion, complete, perfect. — ANANDAMAYI MA

Actually they have got it right. The very fact that it's *you*, you the second-person who are being addressed, you who are invited to par-ticipate in this perfect realization, is enough to shatter the shell of the I and rule out the notion of a wholly Self-centered First Person Singu-lar. Other centers are recognized, taken for granted. Also these pronouncements should not be read out of context. Both of these sages, like all who deserve that title, insist that the Atman or ultimate Subject is also Brahman who is the ultimate Object that deserves total adoration for its own sake. Here is the realm of paradox, where extremes meet and unite. Thus Eckhart, razor-sharp and uncompromising as usual:

> The more God is in all things the more He is outside
> them. The more He is within the more He is without.

So it's not a case of a God who stays or a God who gets away. Not a case of God immanent or God transcendent — which shall it be? — but of both at once. Of two sides of a coin that's worthless and a nonsense till it's indeed two-sided.

In all the great religious traditions there lurks the tendency and temptation to assert one side and deny the other, with unfortunate results. A Deity whose only home is up there in the sky is terribly apt to degenerate into a bigoted and cruel warlord, and one whose only home is down here in my heart is terribly apt to degenerate into a self-worshipping Narcissus. The more unbalanced medieval enthusiasts, Sufi as well as Christian, went the second way. So, as we have suggested, did some Hindu adepts. As for Buddhism, there have been some who took seriously, and even sought to apply to themselves, the charmingly tall story that the Buddha, immediately on emerging from his mother's womb, stood bolt upright and called on Heaven and Earth to witness that he alone was the World-honored One! And for sure none of us is free from the urge to lay hands on our Being and Reality and stick our personal label all over it. Some would attribute this compulsion to the Satan in us who is hell-bent on self-deification in his own right and on his own terms, never mind the fact that to be the One is to vanish in favor of the One. In truth, only Nothing has room for Everything. Only a Nothing that's awake to its nothingness is awake to its Allness. So long as any part of me remains unsurrendered I shall never be Myself.

This essential surrender of the self-that-is-itself to the Self-that-is-Another is surrender *now*. Repeat *now*. According to that preeminent authority on surrender, Jean-Pierre de Caussade, it's the golden key to the treasure house of the present moment:

It is on God's purpose, hidden in the cloud of all that

happens to you in the present moment, that you must
rely. You will find that it always surpasses your own
wishes. The present moment holds infinite riches beyond your wildest dreams.

What makes the now so precious is that it's the moment when one
disappears in favor of the Other. This isn't for blindly believing but for
moment to moment testing with an open mind. How unhelpful here is
Map 1, how misleading when we come to the crucial business of Self-
realization through self-surrender. This for three reasons. First, because it pinpoints a God surrendered to me rather than vice versa, a
Noumenon encapsulated in layer upon layer of phenomena, a Reality
held hostage by its own appearances, Eternity trapped in time. And
second, if "to surrender to" means "to lean on, to rely upon, to take
comfort in, to expand and relax into, to have for backing and sole
resource" (and it does mean all that), then I defy anybody to lean back
on a Point, not to mention explode into a Point! But a Point is all I'm
offered. It's the old story: you can do anything with a bayonet except
sit on it. The third reason why our map won't do is that it's not a map
of the First Person Singular, Present Tense. Quite the contrary, it's essentially time-ridden. And, as we've noted, surrender to the One we
really are is now or never.

Let me enlarge on this third reason why we need a new map. The
old one shows an all-round-the-compass 360-degree world, a world
that takes quite a time to register. For at any one moment the visible
scene ahead of me is restricted to a sector of about 160 degrees, and of
course when I turn around to take in the rest of it I lose that first sector.
In other words, this 360-degree map is a compilation, a useful artifice
which, however, goes far beyond the facts as they are given *now*. Part of
it predates another part, as if Eastern Europe were shown 1914 and
Western Europe were shown 1918. To go by it is to refuse to surrender
to *present* evidence. Refuse to surrender, in particular, to the fact that
never for a moment do I lack this infinite Resource at my back. Curiously enough, one of the circumstances that I'm called on to surrender
to is the fact that I'm neither a crab nor one of those frogs whose eyes
are mounted on stalks, and who presumably enjoy (or is it suffer from?)
360-degree vision. Map 1 would suit them nicely. But not me — fortunately. Unlike "lesser" creatures, humans are all-too-prone to deny their
divine backing, and therefore are lost without the clear evidence of it

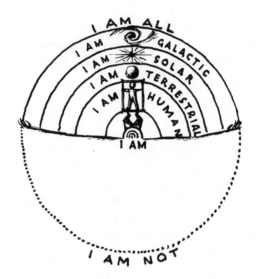

that, mercifully, they are granted. As shown on this revised map.

MAP 2. FIRST PERSON SINGULAR, PRESENT TENSE

To get the flesh out of a grapefruit, halve it. Likewise with our map. See how thoroughly this revised version corrects the faults of the previous one. Though still comfortably ensconced at my center, the ME expands to infinity, thus revealing itself as also NOT-ME, as transcendent-immanent, as graspable and ungraspable. You could say this is having your cake and eating it too, or making the best of both worlds. To put it better, it's as if my tiny rowboat, adrift and at the mercy of time's every current, were suddenly to hoist and unfurl an immense white sail, eternally billowing out with the wind of God. Empowered like this, how can I not ship my oars and submit to that gale?

It came to me late, this new map. Not till my mid-seventies, and long after I had realized the infinite Treasure of the present moment, did I take a deep breath and chop my precious map in two. Ever since then it has served as a wonderfully improved reminder and guide to the marvels of first-personhood, in contrast to the multiple handicaps that mirrored second/third person suffers from. It has gone on to disclose hitherto obscure or unsuspected distinctions between those two sides of me, and how to cope with the ups and downs of their life together. This isn't the place to go into details. You will find some of them discussed elsewhere.

The fact is, of course, that Map 2 is provisional and far from complete. In common with even the best examples of cartography, it needs periodical revision and updating. For this, if for no other reason, it's in little danger of degenerating into a holy icon that discourages adventure instead of stimulating it.

Yes indeed. As recently as a couple of months ago a problem cropped up, which obliged me to revise the map quite drastically. Again, I'm shocked at the delay. I should have tumbled onto the problem years earlier. Map 2 had itself all along been busy rubbing my nose in it.

What prompted this revision was the blazingly obvious fact that whereas one's visible world is restricted to a sector of around 160 degrees, one's audible world is by no means so limited. If I shut my eyes and you creep round me ringing a bell at intervals, I can point with fair accuracy to where the sound is coming from. The bell may be in front of me or behind, to the far left or the far right, my ability to locate it remains unaffected.

It's much the same, of course, with the sense of touch. I can handle and feel the wall at my back in the same way and with the same certainty as anything in front of me.

In short, hearing and touch, unlike sight, are 360 degrees, all-directional senses. But of course their range, in striking contrast to the range of sight, is very narrow. Thunder and tummy rumbles define, more or less, the limits of my audible world. I can see stars and cells, but can't hear them. As for my tangible world, its range is even narrower. This puny arm is its radius.

So I have a problem. I'll put it in Zen terms.

I find here, instead of my human face, my Original Face. Contrasting to the nth degree with that acquired face in my mirror, I have all along found it to be ageless, changeless, timeless, immaculate. No wrinkle has ever lined this perfect complexion. I would have staked my life on the proposition that the essential feature of this Original Face of mine is that it's featureless.

And now this upset! I find my bright and charming Original Face (the adjectives are traditional Buddhist) has a blemish, a patch that's time-ridden and subject to all the chances and limitations and imperfections that the rest is so free of. To put it crudely, I discover that this wonderfully beautiful Face has all along been besmirched by something like a moustache! A weedy zapata, at that!

Here's a challenge, all right!

The challenge, evidently, is to Map 2 and not Map 1, which (in spite of its grievous defects) enfolds sounds and touches, along with sights and smells and tastes, in its unchoosy 360-degree embrace. Which is not to deny, of course, that in other respects Map 2 is incomparably the more valuable. Nor that hitherto, when a serious doubt or difficulty regarding a map has arisen, it has turned out to be nothing of the sort, but instead an enrichment or refinement, heavily disguised. In that case, what is the lesson that this latest problem has up its sleeve for me?

Is it that hearing and touch have special contributions to make to the life of the spirit? If so, what doors onto Reality do they open that are closed to vision? What vital news about our true Nature, what good news that vision is blind to, is implied in the intrusion of these two wide-angle senses — bringing lashings of time and change in their train — into the timeless and changeless realm at the heart of me? Intrusion on a narrow front, but intrusion none the less.

Let's start with hearing.

All my life (and I guess it's the same with you), I've found that some music (far from all, of course) and some poetry (the ring of words when, occasionally, the right man rings them) tell me something about Reality, about the Universe, about Myself. Something not to be missed, something essential that can be told in no other language and by no other means. So that I find myself saying to myself: a Universe that comes up with the powerful rhythms of the music of *The Mission*, with plainsong endings, with some of Mozart's arias, is that kind of Universe. A Universe that sings like that is a Universe that *is* like that. Just as the June rose tells me what kind of January bush — dirty root, thorny stem, dull leaves, and all — it really was, so a Greek folksong such as *Misirlou* tells me what kind of Reality — all horrors notwithstanding — it's coming from. Yes, mysticism without music is deaf. It's not for nothing that the angels are pictured as an orchestra instead of a prayer meeting. The true Beatific Vision is set to music, and the pure in heart shall hear God.

It's much the same with poetry. I can't describe what it is that's missing from What's-so till it's supplied by Robert Frost's *Stopping by Woods on a Snowy Evening*, for instance. But I do know that without this *je-ne-sais-quoi* the Universe isn't itself, isn't all there. I see it as an essential ingredient in the Ananda or Bliss that is itself an essential ingredient in the *Sat-Chit-Ananda,* which is how the Vedantists describe Reality.

So much for hearing. Now for that other 360-degree sense, which is touch.

I can finger the back of the chair I'm sitting in as easily as the front of the table I'm sitting at, and the feel of the one is as real and convincing as the feel of the other. In the same way, but much more importantly, I can finger my head all round: front, back, and sides, the rough and the smooth — all are equally in evidence. It's obvious that invisibility isn't at all the same as non-existence, and that this, for-me-transparent but tangible head is every bit as solid and substantial as that equally transparent but tangible pane of glass in my window.

Yes, the First Person Singular does indeed sport a head — of sorts. The question is: what kind of head, and *in what ways does it differ from all the others?* On present evidence, what is the topography of this Topknot of mine? And of your Topknot too, as you actively join me in the following five-stage investigation. Don't take my word for anything, test it for yourself.

1. Catching hold of my ears, what do I find lurking between them but unbounded and absolutely empty space? Space that's immediately filled by whatever happens to be on show — from a sky full of stars to a postage stamp. However wide my world, this space of mine which takes it in — which becomes it — is wider. And it's a world that I instantly abolish and recreate at will, whereas second and third-persons merely lower and raise tiny flaps of flesh called eyelids, and that's all there is to it. I feel entirely justified, then, on the clearest of present evidence, in calling this amazing topknot my *Cosmic* or *Divine Head*, or even my *God-head*.

2. Next, fingering its features in detail, what I now find here is certainly not the head of a bird or reptile or fish, or any kind of ape or monkey. Beyond doubt, it's a *Human head*.

3. Exploring in still greater detail, I discover a head with all manner of protuberances and hollows and roughnesses which together identify it as Douglas Harding's, as mine uniquely. I call it my *Personal head*.

4. Dropping these busy head-building hands into my lap, I lose all evidence of that thing, or of anything, right here. Instead, I have this awake No-thing which takes in all things, this clear No-head which vanishes in favor of all other heads. This is the way I'm built,

not yet the way I feel and behave.

5. It remains for me to lift my hands from my lap, spread them wide and notice (to my astonishment) that they *embrace* the world in whose favor I disappear, and go on to live accordingly. No easy assignment! It means nothing less than to do consciously what I do anyway, which is to die for my friend, for my enemy, for you. This last stage of the Divine Descent, as our Map 3 indicates, is crucifixion.

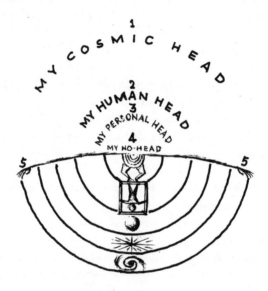

MAP 3. FIRST PERSON SINGULAR, PRESENT TENSE — SHOWING THE FIVE STAGES OF THE DIVINE DESCENT

It is to indicate the immense importance of these five stages, and to record the fact that they are, and feel like, a descent, that Map 3 inverts Map 2.

I'm not saying, mark you, that this third map at last does justice to the Terrain of the First Person. Far from it. I'm fairly certain that better maps will follow, the work of other cartographers. And quite certain that the best of them will be of use only insofar as its user takes on and becomes not only the map but the Terrain itself, and so begins to realize the full splendor of his first-personhood. For it's not by having wonderful thoughts and feelings about one's true Identity that one identifies with it, but by seeing and hearing and touching — repeat touching — this eminently visible and audible and tangible Wonder of Wonders.

What I *am* saying is that this long-time exercise in autocartography — this series of maps — has been my teacher all along. A peculiar guru and not everyone's choice, maybe, but patient, thorough, and in the long term effectual. My only complaint is how slow to learn this disciple has been.

Here, by way of summary and reminder, are the guru's main lessons:

MAP 1 indicates how what I'm perceived to be depends on the distance of my observer. Indicates also the mystery and uniqueness of What, at the Center, is giving rise to all those appearances, and which only I am in a position to view. The defect of Map 1 is that it misrepresents this Central Reality as only central, as immanent and not also transcendent. The Boundlessness there figures as a mere point.

MAP 2 indicates how, in fact, that Reality explodes to infinity without ever leaving the Center, and is at once immanent and transcendent. Relying solely on vision, however, Map 2 fails to take account of other senses.

MAP 3 indicates the privileged role of touch in our enjoyment of the Divine, and its five-stage coming down from the highest height to the lowest depth. It draws attention to that process of Incarnation and Self-giving, which is the very mainspring of the First Person Singular.

LOOK FOR YOURSELF
WORKSHOPS: NEW
TECHNIQUES FOR
REALIZING OLD TRUTHS

Periodically groups of people meet, not to cluster round a guru, not to listen to a lecture, not to meditate, not to discuss any topic, but to take part in an activity called a Look-for-Yourself Workshop. I want to outline here the purpose, the principles, the procedure, and the results of such a workshop.

PURPOSE
The aim of the workshop is that each participant shall turn his attention round to what he is for himself in his own immediate experience. In other words, to what he's looking out of, to how it always is where he always is, to what it's like being First Person Singular, present tense. In more traditional language, the aim is that he should clearly see into his changeless original nature.

PRINCIPLES
The basic idea of the workshop is that we learn by doing, by trying things out, by what we discover actively, rather than by what we read or are told. Experimentation is the name of the game. And it's easier to make discoveries and try things out in a group than individually (1) because most of the experiments involve a number of people anyway, (2) because the members of the group stimulate and encourage one another and make joint discoveries, (3) because it's much easier to concentrate for an hour or two in a group than on one's own, and — not the least important — (4) because it's more fun. A Look-for-Your-

self Workshop is quite unscripted and unpredictable. Everyone is encouraged to participate and anything may happen, so it's an alive occasion, and no one is likely to fall asleep. And, if the workshop works — which it almost always does — nobody goes out of it unable to see into his true nature. Unwilling maybe, unable never.

There has to be a leader, of course. His or her job isn't to impose a program, but to keep people from straying too far from the purpose of the occasion as defined above. However, it's important that no one person should lead workshops: any seer is qualified for the job, and not a few are brilliant at it.

PROCEDURE

Over the past half-century a repertoire of experiments has been devised. Since they are all designed to serve the one purpose of pointing to our original nature, it isn't necessary to work through the lot. Any one of them is sufficient. On the other hand, since people's temperaments are so very different, every workshop, no matter how brief, contains a number of experiments, and it's up to each participant to find out which of them works best for him or her. Thus, differing temperaments are catered for. Moreover, each approach to our central nature confirms and reinforces the others. To come to that essential experience from several directions adds nothing to the experience, but it does emphasize its accessibility and leaves us with no excuse for avoiding any longer the fundamental truth about ourselves.

Two examples will illustrate the sort of experiments that are conducted in a workshop.

The Unclassifiable

A colored sticker — red or green or yellow or blue — is applied to the forehead of each participant by the workshop leader, who tells him to shut his eyes while the sticker is put on. He is forbidden to look in a mirror, or to ask others what his color is, or to tell them what theirs is. The group is then told to sort itself out into four subgroups — all the reds in one corner of the room, all the greens in another, and so on — and to accomplish this sorting, participants may behave as they please, subject only to the rules laid down.

What usually happens is that some wander around futilely trying to guess their color, while others — completely baffled — just give up. Till someone has a bright idea and puts it into operation, and then the four subgroups are swiftly formed and everyone is duly classified.

The threefold lesson of this experiment is that, in and for oneself, one is absolutely unclassifiable, that one contains and registers all groups without belonging to any, and that one is classified and placed in a group *by others*.

You may read and re-read the scriptures that insist you are empty till you know them by heart, you may sit forever at the lotus feet of teachers who tell you that intrinsically you are qualityless, you may sincerely believe that this is so, in meditation you may from time to time feel like this. And it's all water off a duck's back. No business results. But now at last the penny drops, as you stand there utterly vacant and at a loss in the workshop, a no-thing waiting to be taken in and made something of in one of the four groups. Now there's no escaping your true identity as the Unclassifiable Classifier. Or, if you like, the New Adam.

Onion Peeling

A workshop member raises an objection: "All right, I see that *for myself* I'm no-thing. But this could be a subjective delusion. Also relevant, perhaps more relevant, is what I am *for others*. Why shouldn't I go by their impression of me?"

"Why not?" agrees the leader. "But exactly *what* are their impressions of you?" he asks. And proceeds to place the questioner at one end of the room while he, the leader, surveys him from the other end through the viewfinder of a camera or a hole in a sheet of paper. He announces that the view from here — say 20 feet from the questioner — is of a man. But there are other views of the same subject to be had, other appearances to be explored, at other distances. At 10 feet, say, the leader's view is of the top half of a man, from the waist up. Then, coming still closer, of a head, then of an eyebrow or a nose or a mouth, then of a patch of skin, then of a mere blur. And finally, at the point of contact, nothing at all. Which agrees with and confirms the questioner's view of himself at center. And so, in the end, the objective and the subjective accounts of him agree. The outsider's story and the insider's story dovetail neatly.

But why, one may ask, go to the trouble of enacting on the workshop floor what should be plain enough already — the fact that when one goes right up to anything one finds a lot of other things, and in the end nothing at all?

A dear friend of mine once said to me: "For three years or more this idea — that a "thing" is a nest of regional appearances surrounding a central reality which is void — had been familiar and indeed obvious to me. I believed I had fully grasped it, and all the more so because my job in a biological laboratory involves the daily use of a electron microscope. But it was only when I actually took part in the Onion-peeling Experiment that the meaning hit me like a ton of bricks, and I *became* that void."

Incidentally, that friend is now herself an experienced leader of Look-for-Yourself Workshops.

These two random examples of the twenty or so experiments that have so far been devised, some of which rely on other senses than vision will be enough to indicate the sort of thing that goes on in a workshop.

RESULTS

Experience in nineteen countries over the past forty years, conducting workshops lasting from one hour to a week and varying in numbers from two or three to two thousand and more, shows one thing clearly. The interested participant will realize the workshop's purpose and see, however briefly and tentatively, into his true nature. What he will then do with his in-seeing, whether he will go on with it till it becomes quite steady and natural and therefore fully operative, is of course another question. On the face of it the chances are that he will not. On the other hand, it is certain that his flash of insight into the basic truth about himself can only be to the good, and even if he doesn't so much as dream of practicing it, he cannot undo or rid himself of a vision, which is essentially timeless. And sooner or later he may find that above all things he needs to reactivate his own, firsthand discovery of the kingdom and the power and the glory which lie within him.

EPILOGUE

You have looked for yourself and found the treasure. My warmest congratulations! Go on enjoying this vision in ordinary life (grimly practicing it is so much less effective) till it's steady — till it comes quite naturally — and all the rest will be added.

One of the most enjoyable and effectual ways of cultivating your own vision is to share it with others. You can readily do this by carrying out some of our experiments with them. That's to say, by setting up a workshop (another misleading word, but tell me a better one) with one or more friends. And, if you think you aren't ready to hand on what you haven't yet got a grip on, be reassured by this true story of my friend, Pierre.

Pierre, who had practiced *zazen* (sitting meditation) for years, turned up at a workshop and failed to see what it was all about. This is liable to happen when, due to strong past commitments of any kind, a participant's mind, instead of being open, is obstructed with expectations. He was sufficiently intrigued, however, to tell his wife about what had happened in the workshop. Whereupon she immediately saw what he had failed to see, and in turn *showed him!* At last he saw what he had been looking for throughout all that sitting meditation, and his life changed dramatically. Since then he has shared his vision with numerous friends.

The happy truth is that it's impossible to hand on part of the treasure or an inferior version of it. It's an all-or-nothing transaction. Can you think of anything else that, if you do it at all, you do perfectly?

And can you think of any more perfect gift that you can hand to your friends — to the world that needs it so desperately — than this gift of gifts, which you are now fully able to bestow?

THE INNER DIRECTIONS FOUNDATION publishes quality periodicals, books, video, and audio that reflect the heart of nondualistic teachings, from Eastern and Western perspectives.

For additional information, write to:
THE INNER DIRECTIONS FOUNDATION
P.O. Box 231486
Encinitas, California 92023

Phone: 800 545-9118
E-mail: mail@innerdir.org
Website: www.innerdir.org

Books, publications, and workshops of
Douglas E. Harding are available through:
The Shollond Trust
87B Cazenove Road
London N16 6BB
ENGLAND

Phone & Fax: 0181 806 3710
E-mail: headexchange@gn.apc.org
Website: www.headless.org

Additional Publications from The Shollond Trust:
Religions of the World, by Douglas Harding
The Spectre in the Lake, by Douglas Harding
The Science of the 1st Person, by Douglas Harding
Stepping into Brilliant Air, by Colin Oliver
The Headless Way, (Journal of The Shollond Trust)